Garden Pools & Fountains

Created and designed by
the editorial staff of
ORTHO BOOKS

Project Editor
Susan A. Roth

Writer
Edward B. Claflin

Consultant
Charles B. Thomas

Photographer
Saxon Holt

Illustrator
Amy Bartlett Wright

Associate Editor
Pamela Peirce

Designer
Gary Hespenheide

Ortho Books

Publisher
Robert J. Dolezal

Editorial Director
Christine Robertson

Production Director
Ernie S. Tasaki

Managing Editors
Michael D. Smith
Sally W. Smith

System Manager
Katherine Parker

National Sales Manager
Charles H. Aydelotte

Marketing Specialist
Susan B. Boyle

Operations Coordinator
Georgiann Wright

Circulation Manager
Barbara F. Steadham

Administrative Assistant
Kate Rider

Senior Technical Analyst
J. A. Crozier, Jr.

Address all inquiries to:
Ortho Books
Box 5006
San Ramon, CA 94583-0906

Copyright © 1988
Monsanto Company
All rights reserved under international and Pan-American copyright conventions.

17	18	19	20
96	97	98	99

ISBN 0-89721-149-9
Library of Congress Catalog Card Number 87-72812

THE SOLARIS GROUP
2527 Camino Ramon
San Ramon, CA 94583-0906

Acknowledgments

Copy Chief
Melinda Levine

Copyeditor
Frances Bowles

Assistant Copyeditors
Andrea Y. Connolly
Karen K. Johnson

Layout & Pagination by
Linda M. Bouchard

Art Director
Craig Bergquist

Editorial Coordinator
Cass Dempsey

Proofreader
Leslie Cole

Indexer
Frances Bowles

Production by
Studio 165

Separations by
Spectrum Litho, Inc.

Lithographed by
Banta Company

Consultants
Barbara Guarino
  Landscape contractor/designer
  Lilypons Water Gardens
  Lilypons, Md.
Stephene Sheatsley, Barbara Dobbins, co-owners
  Santa Barbara Water Gardens & Landscapes
  Santa Barbara, Calif.
Perry D. Slocum
  Perry's Water Gardens
  Franklin, N.C.

Contributors
Howard Raymond Crum
  Lilypons Water Gardens
  Lilypons, Mass.
Jeffrey B. Hoyt
  Lilypons Water Gardens
  Lilypons, Mass.
Rolf Nelson
  Lilypons Water Gardens
  Brookshire, Tex.

Thanks to Garden Owners
Madeline Bastis, East Hampton, N.Y.
Mitsuko and Andrew Collver, Stony Brook, N.Y.
  (designed and planted garden on pages 6B, 81B, 84L, 88B, 91B)
Lois M. DeDomenico, Piedmont, Calif.
Anthony Diagonale, Wash. D.C.
Nadine Dutcher, Wash. D.C.
Mary Evans, Wash. D.C.
Alexandra Geremia, Santa Barbara, Calif.
Mr & Mrs Clarence N. Goznell, Jr., Potomac, Md.
Faye & Dan Leonard, Silver Springs, Md.
Catherine Mack, Wash. D.C.
Patsy Miller, Potomac, Md.
Tom Normand, Bethesda, Md.
Stephne Sheatsley, Santa Barbara, Calif.
Diane Siegel, Santa Barbara, Calif.
Mr & Mrs Douglas Smith, Wash. D.C.
Jay and Barbara Tracy, Jamestown, R.I.
Michael Zajiic, Wash. D.C.

Photographers
Saxon Holt: Front cover, title page, 4, 6T, 8M, 8B, 9, 10, 12T, 12B, 13T, 13B, 14T, 14B, 15T, 15B, 16, 21, 30T, 30B, 34, 35T, 37, 38, 42, 55B, 56, 57L, 57TR, 57MR, 59TL, 62TL, 62TR, 63BL, 65R, 67L, 68L, 69T, 69B, 70, 72, 76, 78T, 78B, 79M, 79B, 80T, 80B, 81T, 81B, 82, 84R, 85L, 85R, 86L, 86R, 87BL, 87TL, 87BR, 88T, 88B, 89T, 89B, 92L, 92R, 93, 96, 98T, 98B, 99, 100T, 100B, 102, 108, back cover TL, TR, BR.
Stephan Meyers Photography: 35B, 45L, 46L, 46R, 47L, 49L, 49R, 50TR, 50BR, 51TR, 52L, 52R, 58L, 59TR, 59BR, 60TR, 61TL, 64TL, 64BR, 66L, 66R, 67R, 67B, 68R, 73T, 73B
Perry D. Slocum: 40T, 44, 45R, 47R, 48, 51BL, 51R, 53, 54R, 55T, 59BL
Bill Heritage: 7, 29, 40B, 50L, 57B, 58RT, 58RB, 60TL, 63TR
Anita Sabarese: 60BR, 61BR, 61TR, 62B, 63TL, 68B
Susan Roth/The Plant Photo Library: 6B, 18, 84L, 91B, back cover BL
Derek Fell Horticultural Slide Library: 8T, 79T, 87TL, 91T
Laurie Black/Ortho Slide Library: 95T, 95M, 95B
Santa Barbara Water Gardens: 61BL, 63BL
Tom Tracy/Ortho Slide Library: 31, 83
Michael Landis/Ortho Slide Library: 74
Michael McKinley/Ortho Slide Library: 65TL
Amy Bartlett Wright: 75T
Kenneth Rice: 75B

Thanks to Landscape Designers and Architects
Madeline Bastis, Reflections Water Garden Design, Amagansett, N.Y.: Front cover, 18
Grant Castleberg & Associates, Santa Barbara, Calif. Pond designs: 10, 69T, back cover TL
Tony Diagonale and Michael Zajic, Wash. D.C.: 8M, 15T, 30T
Jim Fisher, Landscape Artistry, Inc., Brinklow, Md.: 84R
Alex Geremia, Santa Barbara, Calif. Pond designs: title page, 15B, 56, 69B, 99
Isabelle Greene & Associates, Santa Barbara, Calif. Pond designs: 78T, 81T, 89B
Barbara Guarino, Lilypons Water Gardens, Lilypons, Md.: 16, 21
Hans Hanses, Landscape Architect, Potomac, Md.: 98B
R. J. Lewis Landscape Contractors, Germantown, Md.: 4, 12B, 35T, back cover BR
Tom Normand, Bethesda, Md.: 14B, 72, 89T, 96
Oehme, vanSweden & Associates, Wash. D.C.: 38, 78B, 93
Santa Barbara Water Gardens & Landscapes, Santa Barbara, Calif. Planting designs: title page, 8B, 10, 13B, 15B, 34, 56, 69T, 70, 76, 78T, 79M, 79B, 81T, 82, 89B, 98T, 99, back cover TL, back cover TR. Pond and planting designs: 8B, 12T, 13T, 14T, 70, 80T
Paul Suderburg, Santa Barbara, Calif. Pond designs: 13B, 34, 76, 79B, back cover TR
Michael Zajic, Wash. D.C.: 80B

Front Cover
Growing in this charming garden pool are tropical water lilies, a hardy water lily, pickerel rush, parrot's-feather, water hyacinth, and shellflower. Plants supplied by S. Scherer & Sons, Northport, N.Y.

Back Cover
Top left: The rugged boulders bordering this small garden pool lend a naturalistic feeling to an otherwise formal setting. Top right: In a desert climate, a water garden creates a welcome oasis for plants and people. Lower left: Piped statuary, such as this swan, looks appropriate in a formal pool where it provides a focal point and circulates the water. Lower right: This naturalistic waterfall, built into the existing grade, creates a peaceful setting filled with the soothing sound of running water.

Title Page
Part of the visual pleasure of a water garden comes from playing up the different foliage shapes and textures.

Garden Pools
& Fountains

Using Water In Your Garden

Still or moving water creates a romantic mystique in any garden.

Complete with fountain or waterfall, a garden pool heightens the allure of any garden setting, adding shimmering reflections and flashes of light, glistening movements and sounds of nature. Whether moving or still, water always draws the eye, so that it becomes a focal point in the garden. While contemplating the reflections of blooming water lilies or listening to the splash of a nearby fountain, you'll derive hours of pleasure from a water garden. In a backyard or garden of any size, well-designed water features can turn an ordinary yard or garden into an attractive place to relax and enjoy the outdoors.

The water element may take many styles and forms, from a small, simple fountain with a basin to a large artificial pond fed by a recirculating stream and waterfall. The pond may be bordered with a sweeping brick patio or naturalistically edged with bog plants. Whether dining near a patio pool or strolling along the border of a fish-stocked pond, you will appreciate the moods that water creates. When you view a quiet pool on a warm summer's day, the stillness elicits a feeling of tranquility. The reflections of flowers, leaves, birds, and sky harmonize with the surrounding landscape. Gentle ripples break the water's surface as a breeze plays over the pool, and the glint of gold catches your eye as fish dart beneath the lily pads.

The sound and sight of moving water is both relaxing and entrancing. The steady splash of a fountain or the echoing cascade of a waterfall enhances the pleasure of sitting outdoors. A garden pool can be relaxing and romantic at night. Fragrant night-blooming water lilies scent the air while moonlight sparkles on the water's surface and on foam from a fountain or waterfall.

Naturalistically placed rocks and masses of pink azaleas enhance the green depths of this pretty patio-side pool.

INSTALLATION CONSIDERATIONS

It's not difficult to incorporate a water feature in your garden landscape—you can do it yourself or have one designed by a landscape architect or designer and installed by a landscape contractor. Considering how much a pool or fountain adds to your outdoor environment, the cost is relatively low, especially if you do the installation yourself. Most of the construction materials are available at large garden centers, aquatic nurseries, and hardware stores. A number of specialty mail-order supply houses provide plants, fish, fertilizer, and other supplies for the water gardener.

This book provides detailed instructions for designing and installing garden pools, ponds, fountains, and waterfalls. You will learn about the many lightweight materials—such as flexible PVC liners and prefabricated rigid pools—that make installation easy for do-it-yourselfers. You will learn how to fit the water feature effectively into your garden and discover the abundance of water lilies, aquatic plants, and fish that flourish in water.

Throughout this book you will find photographs of pools, fountains, and waterfalls of many styles, shapes, and sizes. Any of these might fit into your own garden or backyard. The photographs also show the landscaping elements that make water features attractive. You will see how to use water lilies, lotus, and other aquatic plants as well as naturalistic or formal poolside plantings to enhance the pool. A nearby deck or patio, benches, bridges, and stepping stones all make the water garden more accessible. Many possibilities await you—the rest is up to your imagination.

The rest of this chapter offers advice on how to choose the best pool design to fit most attractively into your garden. The remaining chapters provide installation and care instructions. "Installing Your Water Garden" shows, step-by-step, how to prepare your garden site, excavate, and install various types of pools. You will also learn how to install a waterfall and fountain, and learn about pumps and filters. In "Landscaping Your Garden Pool," you will find out how to make your pool look at home on your property. You'll read about the many kinds of edging materials that may be used for bordering the pool and the flowers, shrubs, trees, and ground covers that look best

growing around water. This chapter also contains information on bridges, lights, paths, and sitting areas.

"Planting and Stocking Your Garden Pool" is about the transformation of a garden pool into a water garden. You'll discover how easy it is to plant and grow water lilies and other aquatic plants. And you'll learn about the fish that flourish in a garden pond. In the encyclopedia of aquatic plants included in this chapter, the growth needs of many varieties of aquatic plants are described. The photographs and charts in the encyclopedia will guide you in your final selection. Finally, in "Caring For Your Garden Pool," you will find out how to care for your garden pool so your plants and fish are healthy all year around.

Above: The tall, full jet of this ceramic fountain makes a bold statement that is in keeping with the rugged texture of the wood sides of the raised pool.
Below: The mirrorlike surface of this pool enlarges the garden by reflecting the foliage and flowers of overhead trees and bordering shrubs and perennials.

FORMAL AND INFORMAL POOL STYLES

There are two basic styles of pool design: formal and informal. A formal pool is of a symmetrical or geometric shape such as a circle, square, rectangle, or oval. It looks manmade—but no less lovely—because such uniform shapes aren't often found in nature. An informal pool is irregularly shaped, mimicking nature's own designs.

The most formal kind of pool is one raised and surrounded with brick or stone walls. If mortar or cement work is required, the installation of a raised pool can be a major undertaking that will probably require the help of a builder or landscape contractor. A sunken pool may also have a formal appearance if it is symmetrical in shape and surrounded by a border of paving, walkways, and orderly plantings.

Formal pools and fountains achieved the height of their glory in Renaissance and post-Renaissance architecture, though many are still being built in urban landscapes. The pools in the Tivoli Gardens and at Versailles and the Trevi Fountain in Rome are all examples of formal design. In Japanese and Middle Eastern architecture, formal pools are often an integral part of house and garden design. Many city parks, squares, and plazas in the United States feature formal pools and fountains that provide restful settings for lunchtime strollers.

The clear-cut lines of formal pools are often in keeping with the neat appearance of a town house or large period-style house. They look at home among neatly pruned shrubs and trees, in the middle of an expanse of lawn, or as a focal point in a town house garden.

The materials, such as cut stone, paving block or brick that are used to surround formal pools are themselves round, square or rectangular. A tall fountain jet or piped statuary becomes the focal point of the formal water garden. Waterfalls should also be symmetrical, in clean-cut steps with the water falling in sheets.

Water lilies and lotus can be used to decorate the water surface. If plants form the margin of a formal pool, they are best kept in neat beds, to expose the clean lines of the pool's edge. The effect is that of a well-planned and well-ordered garden.

The far-reaching spray of this cherub fountain glimmers in the sun and plays on the surface of the water like splashing raindrops.

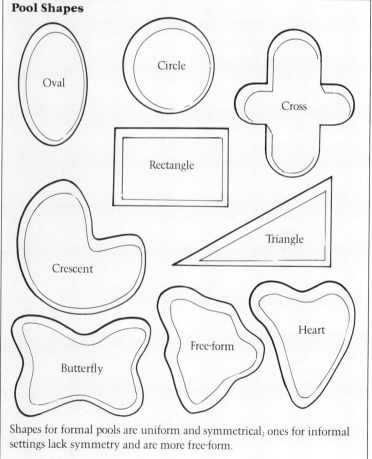

Pool Shapes

Oval

Circle

Cross

Rectangle

Triangle

Crescent

Free-form

Heart

Butterfly

Shapes for formal pools are uniform and symmetrical; ones for informal settings lack symmetry and are more free-form.

Informal pools have irregular shapes and usually resemble natural ponds. They look perfectly at home near a rambling country house or a farmhouse or in a treed suburban yard. Bordered by naturalistically placed stones and planted with overhanging ferns, tall grasses, iris, or wildflowers, the shoreline melts into the surrounding landscape. Bog and other aquatic plants often grow in the pool, creating a true water garden. A path, patio, or deck bordering one edge will provide access to an informal pool without spoiling its natural character. Unlike the formal pool that looks man-made, an informal pool looks as if it were a part of the natural landscape.

As a general rule, gardeners should choose one style or the other but not try to combine both. A formal pool is ideal for a patio, deck, or terrace that has clean, symmetrical lines; it looks appropriate in front of a garden wall. Informal pools are better suited to naturalistically planted landscapes and to lawns with wooded backdrops. Although highly experienced gardeners have occasionally combined both styles in a single setting, a pleasing effect is difficult to achieve. Usually, the combination of formal and informal elements is more disturbing than pleasing.

When choosing a style for your water garden, consider how its design will complement the style of your garden and the architecture of your house. A pond filled with aquatic plants and surrounded by bog plants can bring the great outdoors into your backyard. But it should look natural in its setting, perhaps with tall trees as a distant backdrop. A symmetrical pool with a tall fountain jet looks better at the edge of a patio or linked by a wide walk to the house, than in a natural woodland setting. Think about the garden as it is and try to imagine how the water feature will fit in.

POOL SIZE, SHAPE, AND DEPTH

A number of factors influence the size of a garden pool. Most important is the scale of your garden. A small, fenced-in garden can be overwhelmed by a pool that looks too large for the space available; a very small pool will look lost in an open expanse of landscape.

When choosing a water feature for your garden, you must first consider the amount of space you have available. No area is too large or too small for a pool or fountain, but the space and feature must complement each other. For instance, to accent an enclosed patio, a trickle fountain in a small pool looks perfect. Surrounded by a low-growing border of spring bulbs and summer annuals, the pool

Above: Rocks play an important role in a naturalistic setting; here boulders create the realistic look of tiers of waterfalls. Opposite above: A small, brick-edged pool harmonizes in material and formality with this courtyard of a city garden. Opposite center: In a formal setting a waterfall that drops in a thick sheet looks and sounds dramatic. Opposite below: A trickle of water emerging from a pile of rocks adds the movement and sound effects that create a naturalistic touch.

cover as much as 6 to 12 square feet of water surface. If you expect to cultivate a large number of water lilies, remember that most varieties will spread widely across the pond during the growing season.

This spreading benefits fish, since they need the shade, and the reduced sunlight slows algae growth. However, you need to decide how many water-surface plants you would like to grow, then allow sufficient area for their spread in summer. In temperate zones, surface plants will die back during the winter, leaving the full expanse of the pond exposed to view. (See pages 39 to 75 for more details on fish and aquatic plants.)

Around the edges of an informal pool, you may want to grow plants that are leafy, grass-like, or flowering. Their leaves and stems stand above the surface of the pool and take up much less room on the surface of the water than water lilies.

An informal pool may be adjoined by a boggy area set aside for plants that prefer wetness around their roots. In a bog garden, the water is cupped in a shallow liner that is covered by moist, heavy soil. It is an ideal place to grow some of the moisture-loving plants that flourish around ponds. If the bog adjoins the pool and shares its water supply, you will have to plan this area when you design your garden pool. Otherwise the bog area can be added later (see page 83).

As well as considering the size and position of a garden pool, you also need to think about the shape. In a naturalistic garden, the pond should fit into the terrain, hugging the bends and curves of a hillside or echoing the outline of your property or garden beds. Even in a formal setting, you may want to reflect the curving borders of a terrace with a round pool or the straight lines of a deck with a rectangular pool.

With flexible pool liners your choice of size and design is unlimited—the pool becomes your own creation. Preformed pools made of fiberglass, bonded resin, or plastic range in size from about 4 feet by 3 feet (100 gallons) to approximately 9 feet by 8 feet (420 gallons) and come in many regular and irregular shapes. An artificial pool can be of any dimension, but the style you select should complement the design of your house and garden so that it looks attractive in its surroundings.

becomes a lovely centerpiece for the intimate patio setting. A larger pool would make the area seem crowded. Almost any open, grassy area worn down by constant foot traffic would be an ideal place for a naturalistic lily pond with a walkway around the edge.

On a large property there are nearly limitless possibilities—both formal and informal. But the size of the garden pool should be in keeping with the setting. A wide-open space calls for a grand pool. You might like the effect of several natural-looking, irregularly shaped ponds linked by gently flowing streams and waterfalls. Or for clean, elegant lines, you might select a perfectly round formal pool with a tall fountain jet in the center. Instead of garden beds, surround the pool with a brick terrace and add a few benches.

You also want to consider the kinds of plants you will grow, since some take up a much larger surface area than others. Even the medium-size varieties of water lilies may

Pool Depth

It is unnecessary to have continually flowing fresh water in a garden pool in order to keep the water clear. But you do need to have enough water in the pool so that plants and fish will have a healthy environment. Together they inhibit the growth of competing algae. In general, the water is clearer and more reflective in a deep pond than it is in a shallow pond.

Mapping Out the Design

When deciding where to place your pool and what size it should be, you will find it helpful to visualize the finished pool. Map out the pool with a garden hose or rope, changing its situation, size, or shape until you are pleased with the effect. It helps to stand back and even look out from a nearby window to get a good idea of what the finished pool will look like. When you've made a decision, observe the area to see how much sunlight it gets every day. (Most water lilies need a minimum of six hours of sunlight each day.) Then draw a plan, to scale, on graph paper. This step is especially important if you intend to install walkways, benches, or other elements after the pool is finished. The plan will show whether you have allowed enough space for the surrounding features.

SITE REQUIREMENTS

Before beginning to dig, be sure that the site is suitable for a garden pool. When selecting a site, take into account the soil type, drainage, the amount of sunlight, and access to water and electricity.

Topography

Good grading to allow for drainage is essential. A pool should not be placed so that runoff from the surrounding landscape will drain into it; this is especially important if fertilizers and pesticides are used in the garden nearby. If the pool is placed in a low-lying area (where it looks most natural) be sure to include a diversion course so that the surface water will be directed around the pool, not into it.

The soil itself should be well drained. Although it might seem natural to have a pool in a low-lying or swampy area, this is actually the worst place to choose. Boggy, wet soil can

A border of irregular stones and the curve of a wooden bridge soften the straight lines of this small, formal pool. Aquatic plants include the hardy water lilies 'Comanche' (apricot and yellow) and 'Gladstone' (white), water hawthorn, and iris.

heave the bottom of an artificial pool, cracking or breaking it and, during a heavy rain, water that has drained down to the pool area will lift up the liner. Any flooding in the vicinity will cause leaves and soil to sluice over the edge of the pool, adding silt and decaying matter to the fresh water in the pond.

If your soil is very sandy or crumbly, you will also have problems. To keep the soil from caving in, you will have to design a pool with gently sloping sides or use flat stones as retaining walls.

If you have doubts about your soil, check it by digging a hole about 24 inches deep before you begin making extensive plans. If the soil has many large rocks or pebbles in it, plan on lining the excavation—walls and bottom—with several inches of sand in order to level it out and prevent puncturing the liner. (See pages 20 to 26 for details.)

Sun Requirements

The next consideration is sunlight. Most water lilies bloom best when they receive between 10 and 12 hours of bright sunlight a day during the summer. Six hours of direct sunlight a day is the minimum for most water lilies, though a few varieties bloom with only four hours of direct sun. If you want to grow water lilies or lotus, place your pond in full sun; if not, a shadier spot is usually fine, though your choice of other aquatics will be more limited. However, it's generally best to choose a situation as far as possible from the overhanging limbs of trees. Decaying leaves on the pond's bottom can be lethal to fish and plant life, because they rob the water of oxygen and make the water too acid. Fallen leaves have to be cleared frequently during autumn. When they sink to the bottom of the pool, they can clog pumps and filters.

You can install water features even if conditions are not ideal. In fact, a woodland filled with trees may be the most picturesque place for a still pool or a gently flowing stream. Although you cannot grow water lilies in full shade, there are many other kinds of flowers, ferns, ground covers, and shrubs that will flourish around a sheltered pool or meandering watercourse. If you don't mind the higher maintenance, there is nothing to prevent you from putting a water feature in the shade, providing that the drainage is adequate.

Right: Viewing this pool from the picture window is a year-round pleasure. Aquatics include creeping water primrose, water hawthorn, parrot's-feather, pickerel rush, narrow-leaved cattail, marsh marigold, water poppy, 'Sunrise' and 'Comanche' hardy water lilies, and 'Panama Pacific' tropical water lily. Below: Water lilies bloom freely in full sun. These are hardy lilies 'Chromatella', 'Fabiola', and 'Gladstone'.

Viewing the Pool

Visually, the ideal place for a pool is close enough to the house so that you can view the water and wildlife from a window. A clear vista of the garden pool from the living room, dining room, or kitchen allows you to enjoy the seasonal changes of trees, flowers, and sky reflected on the surface of the pond even when you haven't time to sit outdoors. And if hot, cold, or rainy weather keeps you inside, the pool can be viewed from indoors. If the pond is lit at night, the effects when seen from inside are brilliant no matter what the weather. A garden pool easily seen from indoors is a pool enjoyed every day of the year.

A pool can appear to increase your patio area or garden size, depending on how it is placed. A long, narrow pool creates the illusion of greater distance; you can make a confined garden look larger than it actually is if you site the pool so that you look down its length. If you plant tall shrubs or trees on the far side of a pool, their reflections in the water also stretch out the distance.

Electricity and Water Supply

In siting a garden pool, you also need to consider how you are going to get electricity and water to it. Fountains and waterfalls obtain their water supply from an electrical pump that sucks up and recirculates pond water. A recirculating pump operates on normal household current, and you will want to be able to

Right: Where a pool poses a danger to infants, try growing water lilies in a tub garden. Many small-spreading varieties of water lily, including this 'Attraction', flourish in containers. Below: When viewed from one end, this long, narrow pool catches the reflections of distant trees and bordering plants and creates the illusion of great distance. The aquatics, recently planted, include cattail, pickerel rush, parrot's-feather, and water lilies.

plug in the pump without a lot of trouble. It is easiest to use an electrical outlet installed on the side of the house or accessible through a garage or basement window. For aesthetics' sake, the electric cable—one designed for outdoor use—leading from the outlet to the pump can be buried under soil or covered by stones. A long cable buried inside a conduit can reach a pump some distance from your house.

You can fill a pool of any size from a hose; no permanent water supply is needed. You will be using a hose not only for the initial filling but also for topping up the water as it evaporates. In summer, evaporation can be quite rapid. If the pool can be easily and conveniently filled from a faucet on the side of your house, your job will be easier. Otherwise, you may want to install underground pipes and a spigot near the pool.

SAFETY

Families with young children must also consider the hazards of installing any garden pool. Even shallow water can be dangerous for infants, who are naturally attracted to ponds and fountains. It would be wise to postpone building a ground-level pool until children are older and can understand the hazards of water. In the meantime, you might consider a bubble fountain falling over a pebbled area that camouflages a grating underneath (see page 32). Or install a trickle fountain merely for the sound effects.

Zoning Laws and Fence Codes

Before beginning a permanent installation, talk to a local building inspector or consult your local zoning ordinances to make certain that there are no special requirements. Do this ahead of time, instead of finding out too late that the size or design of your pool needs to be altered to meet regulations. In some cases, pools cannot be installed without permits, though small garden pools may be exempt. You might have to put up a wall or fence to meet regulations if a garden pool is deeper than a certain depth, which is 18 inches in many communities.

FINISHING TOUCHES

Both formal and informal pools are best edged with rocks or paving to keep the liner in place and camouflage the edges. When choosing materials for the border—called coping—keep in mind the style of your pool. Edgings suitable for naturalistic settings include large rocks, gravel, and smooth fieldstones. Materials for paved sitting areas might include crazy paving (irregularly cut paving fitted together in a random pattern), pebbles set in concrete, or square paving slabs interspersed with plants, soil, and pebbles. For the best effect, choose gray, brown, tan, or black stones, rather than white or colored ones. (See the chapter "Landscaping Your Garden Pool," for more details.)

The border of a formal pool may be constructed of any paving material, such as brick, regular paving stone, or tile, that creates a symmetrical margin. Symmetrical patterns around the border may be continued along the sides and bottom of a concrete pool. (If the water is clear, the patterns are visible to the viewer.) Ceramic or colored tiles are also appropriate around the edges of a formal pool.

Water lilies or lotus plants enhance the mystique of a garden pool. It is important to plant the banks of an informal pool to make it look natural. You may want the entire shoreline to be hidden by bog plants interspersed with boulders, large stones, or gravel, but it's often best to keep one side unplanted so that the pond won't appear too closed in. This open side may be used as a sitting area and be either grassed or paved.

Several types of gardens create pleasant settings for naturalistic garden pools. A bog garden bordering the pool makes a perfect spot for growing plants that need constant water around their roots. But you might prefer a small waterfall, with or without a stream, feeding the pool and running through a rock or wildflower garden. Flowering perennials, ferns, or low shrubs also make attractive plantings. In a spacious pool, you might try placing a large rock so that it juts above the water, creating a natural-looking island.

Bridges, Paths, and Terraces

Since the water garden becomes the center of attention in any garden, you'll naturally want to provide access to it. A bridge spanning a pool or stream makes an attractive vantage point from which a stroller can admire the fish and aquatic plants. Many designs are possible: wooden bridges, with or without

Above: Form and texture are important elements in this stunning arid-climate landscape. The irregularly cut desert-colored fieldstones and the sculptural plantings make a perfect naturalistic border for the pool. Below: This handsome stone-slab bridge links a path leading from the house through the flower garden to the pond-side deck.

Above: A comfortable bench provides a restful spot to relax while enjoying the splash of the fountain and waterfall. In the pool are goldfish and a yellow-flag iris. Below: Almost too pretty to walk on, this stone path runs the length of the raised pool, emphasizing its long lines as well as providing close-up viewing. Garden plants include thyme, coralbells, marguerite, statice, sweet alyssum, sea lavender, and viola, with creeping fig on the wall.

railings, stone slabs, and stepping stones. The proportions of any bridge should be carefully weighed in relation to the size of the pool, the scale of the landscape, and the background setting.

For a short span across a stream or waterfall, a simple stone or granite slab makes an attractive bridge. Though difficult to install because of its weight, a slab bridge creates an impressive sense of permanence.

Stepping stones are very effective in a natural pool of sufficient size. Instead of setting the stones in a straight line, consider staggering them so that they form a pleasing pattern on the water surface. You can use irregular, flat-topped, concrete paving slabs, sections of wooden deck, or boards set on pilings.

A sitting area that may be as simple as a stone or wooden bench, or something as grand as a large patio or deck is also an asset. A dramatic viewing platform can be created by extending a deck or terrace over the edge of the water. Lily pads drifting under the edge of the deck and fish swimming out from beneath the planks enhance the water landscape for anyone sitting on the platform. The deck makes a perfect platform for sitting or dining by the edge of the water.

In planning the areas around your water garden, imagine the different perspectives that a viewer can enjoy from various vantage points. A path around the entire pool allows a visitor to view the plants and water from many different angles, and it gives you easy access to the water garden when you need to do maintenance work. Many attractive materials can be used for permanent walkways and paving, including bricks, quarry tiles, Belgian blocks, cobbles, pebbles, sandstone, terracotta tiles, or wooden blocks set in gravel. In a wooded setting, a path of shredded bark looks perfect and is easy to install.

With a formal pool, dimension will be added by the paving—stone slabs, bricks, or decking—that you set around the edge. Usually, this border would be at least 12 inches wide, though you may want it considerably wider. If you decide to have a flagstone path or patio adjacent to the pool, the area that you require may be extensive. If you're intending to host outdoor parties, plan to have enough space for a table and chairs and leave people enough room to walk about. However, to create the right visual scale, a deck or patio should be no more than three to four times the size of the water garden.

Decks and terraces that will be used for sitting, dining, or viewing should take advantage of the best view. In siting a patio, consider how the area might be used at different times of the day. Watching the evening sun set over a lovely pool adorned with lotus blossoms and lily pads can be a memorable experience, but on a hot summer's afternoon, you might prefer to be seated under some shade, where the glare of the sunlight is not so intense. Ideally, the setting of a garden pool invites the visitor to survey it from a number of natural viewing areas (see pages 91 to 93). You will want to walk and sit beside the water or observe it from indoors while you work.

Installing Your Water Garden

With just a few materials, you can create a beautiful backyard water garden.

I t is not difficult to install a pond and waterfall if you follow the plans included in this chapter. After carefully reading the instructions given here, you can proceed with confidence. All the work described can be done with a minimum of supplies and with a few basic home gardening tools. Unless you are planning a very large pond or some major landscape renovations, you probably won't need to hire an outside contractor.

All the projects described here can be done by one or two people. Excavations require a strong, physically fit person, especially if the soil is heavy or rocky. You might consider hiring someone to do the digging if you aren't up to this much physical labor. Even when building a small pond, you will discover that you dig up suprisingly large quantities of soil. Be prepared to cart the soil somewhere nearby or make arrangements to have it hauled away. If you plan to install a waterfall leading down to the pond, you can use all the soil from the excavation to raise or alter the natural grade of the land.

Here you will also find information on installing pumps and piping for a fountain or waterfall (see pages 34 to 37). And there are instructions for filling the pool and treating tap water (see page 28) so it is suitable for fish and aquatic plants.

Once the garden elements are in place, you will have to add the most essential ingredient of all—patience. It takes time for a water garden to establish a natural ecological balance. Gradually, as a balance is established, surface plants bloom and spread across the water, submerged plants begin to thrive, and murky water becomes clearer. Watching these final changes will be as satisfying as all the excavation and planning that precede them.

An important step in preparing an excavation for a PVC-lined pool is to ensure that the edges are level.

EXPENSE

Unless you are excavating a very large pond or building an extensive patio alongside the pool, you will probably be able to do the installation yourself at a minimal cost. Today, there are many kinds of lightweight, inexpensive pool liners. The most readily available are made of flexible PVC (polyvinyl chloride, a plastic material) or rigid, prefabricated fiberglass, which is somewhat more expensive. Whether you decide to use either of these liners, or choose the more difficult task of installing a concrete pool (the most expensive and permanent choice), your fixed costs can be calculated in advance by knowing the depth and dimensions of the pool, waterfall, or fountain that you want to install.

Apart from the cost of the liner, projected expenses should include the costs of:

☐ Builder's sand to line the excavation
☐ Submersible pump and electric cable
☐ Fountain or decorative fountain head
☐ Permanent pipe for fountain or waterfall
☐ Lights and wiring, if desired
☐ Quarried or precut border materials, such as stone or brick
☐ Dry mortar mix
☐ Aquatic plants and containers
☐ Fish
☐ Miscellaneous supplies for water treatment and plant and fish care.

Unless you undertake extensive masonry or electrical work, you will need only common garden and workshop tools. Excavation can be done with a pick and shovel. For laying out and excavating the pool, you will need a heavy rope or garden hose, one or two straight boards and a spirit level, and stakes of various sizes. Once the pool is installed, the plant, fish, and water maintenance can be done with very little specialized equipment.

The total cost of your pool will depend on the size and your specific plans for walkways, patios, terraces, and ornamentation. However, there are no hidden costs in caring for a pool, fountain, or waterway. Once you have filled the pool, you do not need to use any more water except for occasional topping up. A fountain or waterfall is operated by a recirculating pump that uses very little house current, so a constant flow of water can be maintained at little expense.

POOL MATERIALS

The first decision to be made is whether you want a pool made with a flexible liner, a prefabricated shell, or of concrete. Before the age of plastics, nearly all garden pools were made of concrete. Some homeowners still prefer the substantial quality of a permanent concrete pool. You can easily install a drain in the bottom of a concrete pool. The pool may be inset with decorative ceramic tiles. Concrete may also be sculpted into naturalistic rocklike formations to create a streambed or waterfall.

However, most do-it-yourselfers choose the lighter materials rather than concrete. Their use enables you to build a pool or fountain without skilled labor and great expense, and they are durable, easy to handle, and quick to install. They are also easier to remove if you wish to alter your landscape.

Flexible liners and prefabricated shells come in various colors, including gray, black, and green. Initially, black gives a greater sense of depth and is more easily camouflaged around the edges. However, color should not be a decisive factor in choosing a material. After the plants are established and some desirable mosslike algae has grown along the sides, it is impossible to tell the original color of the pool lining.

Installing a PVC-lined pool is a do-it-yourself project. Two people installed this charming pool during one weekend. Aquatic plants include 'Comanche' hardy water lily, parrot's-feather, shellflower, pickerel rush, lizard's tail, and white snowflake.

Other factors to be considered are cost and durability. Prefabricated pools are considerably more expensive than pools with flexible liners, but they are more durable and less likely to be punctured. Either can be repaired if leaks occur, but a pond must be drained and dried before the shell or liner can be patched.

Consider also the slope or grade of the site. On sloping ground a rigid pool may be better. A flexible liner placed on fresh fill may shift and tear when the soil settles. If you want to use a flexible liner on a slope, it is preferable to excavate to the low point of the site rather than try to fill in dirt on the downhill side.

A concrete pool properly constructed can last for generations but, if the initial construction is flawed, leaks can occur almost immediately. In cold climates the concrete should be lined with wire mesh and reinforcement rods, and walls should be at least 6 inches thick. (Further details of concrete construction are provided on page 29.)

Once installed, pools with flexible liners and those with prefabricated shells look much the same. But several factors may influence your choice between the two. Flexible liners cost less per square foot than do prefabricated pools, and are more versatile since they can be cut and fitted to any size or dimension. A flexible liner allows you to create a pool of whatever shape fits best into your garden. Although flexible liners come in standard lengths and widths, you can seal the pieces together with bonding glue. Some suppliers will do this sealing for you if you specify the dimensions.

With a prefabricated pool you are limited to the shapes and dimensions available from commercial suppliers. The possibilities include formal round, rectangular, and teardrop-shaped pools as well as an assortment of more natural-looking, irregular shapes. Sizes range from 40 to 600 gallons (4 to 35 square feet of surface). Many come with built-in shelves around the edge for holding plants. If you intend to use a prefabricated pool, obtain measurements from your supplier before you finalize your site plans.

Sloping Sites

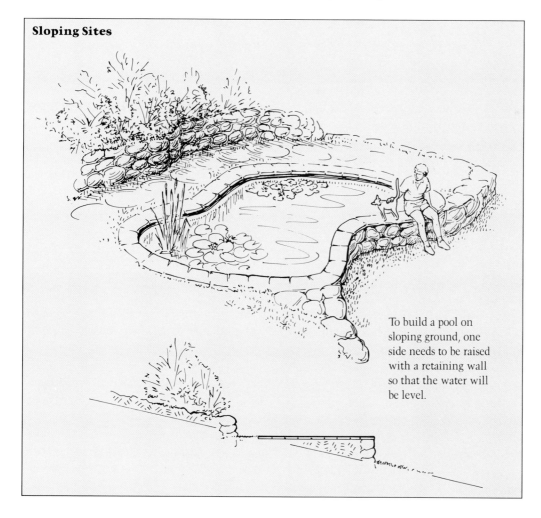

To build a pool on sloping ground, one side needs to be raised with a retaining wall so that the water will be level.

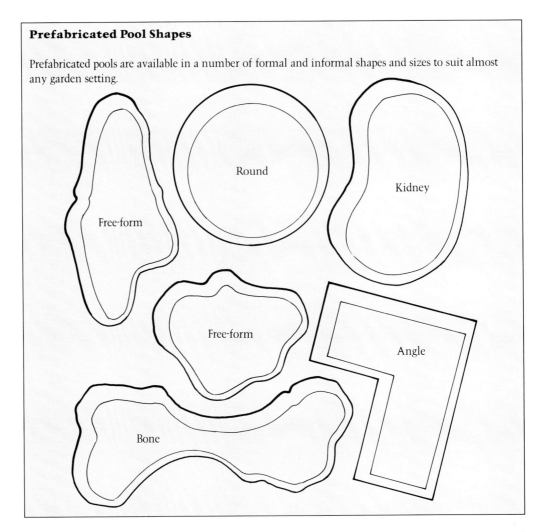

Prefabricated Pool Shapes

Prefabricated pools are available in a number of formal and informal shapes and sizes to suit almost any garden setting.

When you have decided on a material, review the section in this chapter describing how to excavate the site and install the pool. Procedures for installing flexible and rigid liners differ. You will also find it helpful to read through the entire section before you finalize your plans or begin ordering materials.

POOL DEPTH

In general, the water is clearer in a deep pond than it is in a shallow pond. A shallow, saucer-shaped pool is likely to become clouded with excess algae much more quickly than will a deep, steep-sided pool that holds more water. In a small pool there is very little movement of water, so algae spreads rapidly once it begins to grow. Additionally, the water heats up more quickly in a shallow pool, and algae flourish in warm, sunlit water. Submerged plants, floating plants, and fish are usually most successful in a large volume of water.

A pool should never be less than 15 inches deep; 18 inches is preferable. For a 40-square-foot pool (8 feet by 5 feet) the recommended depth is between 18 and 24 inches. Any pool with between 100 and 200 square feet of surface area should be at least 24 inches deep. A body of water larger than 200 square feet need not be more than 24 inches deep.

INSTALLING A FLEXIBLE LINER

Flexible PVC (polyvinyl chloride) is the material most often recommended for lined pools. It is commonly available in several thicknesses. A gray 20-mil single-ply, a 32-mil double-ply that is green on one side and black on the reverse, and a black 30-mil double-ply are good, durable choices. PVC is also available in a 16-mil thickness; this would be the minimum thickness if you want easy, long-lasting construction.

Buy the lining material from a garden center or water-gardening supply house to ensure that it is fish-grade PVC—ask if you are unsure. Other kinds of PVC may be unsuitable.

PVC designed for swimming pool coverings contains chemicals that retard algae growth; however, these chemicals may kill other kinds of plants as well.

If you need PVC in large or unusual sizes, you can splice the sheets yourself or order them specially from the manufacturer. If you decide to do the sealing yourself, use a glue specified for flexible PVC. The PVC glue sold in most hardware stores is for rigid PVC pipe and, unless applied with extreme care, it will burn a hole through the flexible liner.

The main drawback to PVC is that it deteriorates very rapidly if exposed continuously to ultraviolet light (sunlight). However, as long as you keep your pool well filled (which it should be for the sake of plants and fish), the edges will be protected by water and the liner will last a long time. The life of 20-mil PVC is about ten years; the 32-mil variety will last longer. Both will last even longer if protected from direct sunlight. When the material finally deteriorates, it becomes brittle and can no longer be repaired. However, as long as it remains flexible, PVC can be easily repaired with a PVC patching glue (see pages 102 to 103 for details).

Butyl rubber, recommended in many British gardening books, has only recently become available in this country, and may still be

Pool Installation Tools

Before beginning to dig, be sure you have all the tools you'll need in order to do a proper job. The following check list indicates every item to have at hand.

- ☐ Framing square (if the pool is to be square or rectangular)
- ☐ Garden spade
- ☐ Long, straight board (8 feet long or the width of the pool excavation)
- ☐ Pick and crowbar (if the soil is rocky)
- ☐ Rope or garden hose (for laying out the circumference of the pool)
- ☐ Spirit level (12 inches or longer)
- ☐ Stakes
- ☐ String
- ☐ Tarpaulin or ground cover (on which to pile soil)
- ☐ 3- to 4-foot-long board or straightedge to level the edges or diagonals
- ☐ Wheelbarrow or garden cart

difficult to find in some areas. This black rubbery material is 30 mil thick and doesn't degrade in sunlight. A butyl rubber liner should last for forty years or more, but it is about twice as expensive as PVC and more difficult to repair. Installation procedures are the same for any type of flexible liner.

Before installing the PVC liner, a cushioning layer of moist sand must be spread on the bottom of the excavation to protect the liner from punctures.

Installing a Flexible Liner

Before digging, outline the shape of the pool with rope or a garden hose, adjusting it until it looks correct.

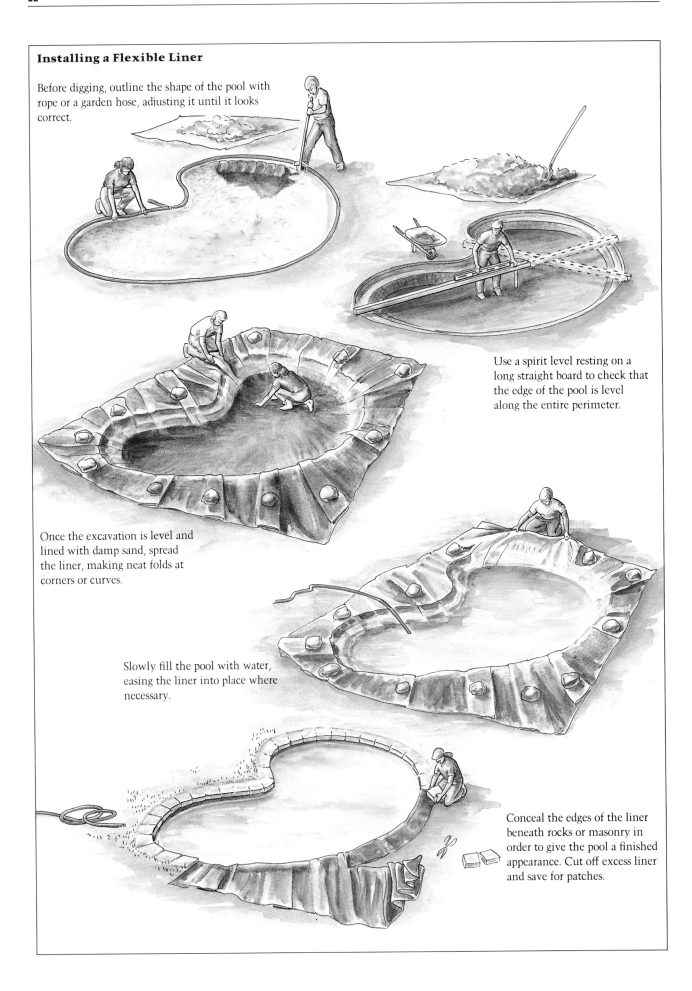

Use a spirit level resting on a long straight board to check that the edge of the pool is level along the entire perimeter.

Once the excavation is level and lined with damp sand, spread the liner, making neat folds at corners or curves.

Slowly fill the pool with water, easing the liner into place where necessary.

Conceal the edges of the liner beneath rocks or masonry in order to give the pool a finished appearance. Cut off excess liner and save for patches.

Steps for Installing a Flexible Liner

There are seven basic steps to the installation of a flexible liner.

1. Outline the pond with rope or garden hose.
2. Measure the pond and buy the liner.
3. Excavate the pond site.
4. Level the top edges of the excavation.
5. Line the excavation with damp sand.
6. Install the liner.
7. Secure the liner with edging or coping.

Step 1: Outline the pond Outline the shape of your pond with a heavy rope or garden hose. Stand back and view the site from several angles and from indoors to be sure the pond is in the right place and of the size and shape that will look best. Adjust the outline until you're satisfied, then stake the rope at 1-foot intervals in case the marker moves when you are digging. For square or rectangular pools, use stakes and string to make sure that the sides are straight. At the corners, measure the 90-degree angles with a large framing square to make sure that they are square.

Step 2: Measure the liner A flexible liner must be large enough to fit the excavation site and overlap the top edges. To figure out how wide a liner you need to buy, measure the pool across its widest dimension and, to that figure, add twice the depth. To calculate the length, measure the longest dimension and, again, add twice the depth. It is unnecessary to allow extra depth for shelves around the edge, since the measurement for the depth will be the same with or without shelves. Add another 1 foot to both the length and the width to make sure you have enough overlap around the edges. Any excess material can be trimmed later and saved for patching.

For example, if your pool is 8 feet long at the surface, 6 feet wide, and 1½ feet deep, you would calculate the length and width of PVC liner thus:

8' + 2 (1.5') + 1' = 12' long
length of pool + twice the depth + surplus for overlap = length
and
6' + 2 (1.5') + 1' = 10' wide
width of pool + twice the depth + surplus for overlap = width

As these calculations show, for a 6-foot by 8-foot pool that is 18 inches deep, you should purchase a 12- by 10-foot sheet of PVC.

If your garden center or mail-order supplier does not carry the size you need, inquire whether it can be made to order. Usually, this can be done without much delay.

Step 3: Excavate the pond site If your pond will be situated in a lawn, begin by stripping off the sod. Pile this in the shade, since you may want to reuse some of it later around the pool edge. Dig the hole to the exact shape of the pool, adding 2 extra inches to the depth to accommodate a layer of sand. Pile the excavated soil on a tarpaulin or in a wheelbarrow.

The pool walls should have a slope of about 20 degrees, or more if the soil is loose or sandy. You can dig marginal shelves about 9 inches wide, positioned between 9 and 12 inches below the top edge of the pool. Shelves can be excavated all around the perimeter of the pool or only on the sides you intend to plant. Some gardeners like to place rocks or flat stones on the marginal shelves both below and protruding above the waterline as a natural-looking edging. If you plan to do this, allow for the dimensions of the rocks when excavating.

If you are bordering the pool with flat fieldstones, dig a small trench along the pool edge so that the stones may be set flush with the surrounding ground. The liner will extend under and behind the stones and you'll be able to bring the water level right up to them.

Excavation Edges

The edges of the pool should slope gently, at about a 20-degree angle. To create a shelf to hold marginal plants, dig a 9-inch-deep by 9-inch-wide shelf along the perimeter.

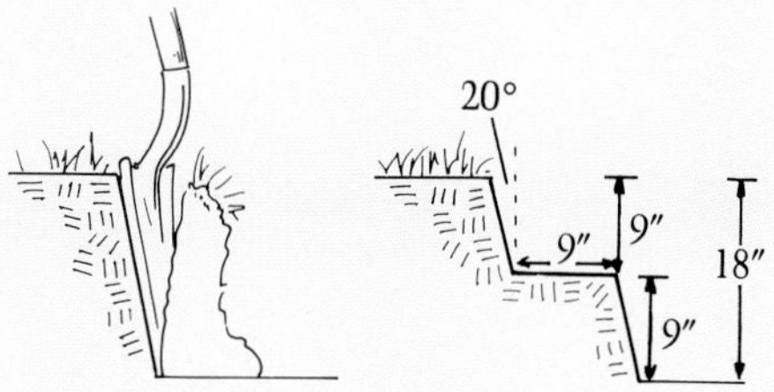

Leveling the Excavation

In a large excavation, check the level by resting one end of a long board on a stake in the center of the pool. Use the stake as a pivot as you check the level at frequent intervals around the perimeter.

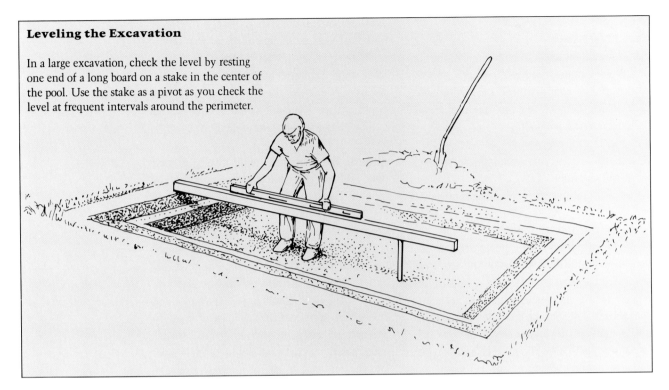

When you have finished digging, remove any rocks that might puncture the liner, then smooth out the soil. Dips or protrusions in the soil can create a weak area when the liner is filled with water.

Step 4: Level the top edges Make sure the top edges of the pool are level. If one edge is lower than the other, the liner on the high side will always be visible and unsightly unless camouflaged with rocks or stones. Getting the edges level may take some time, especially on an irregular grade.

Leveling is done with a spirit level set on top of a straight board spanning the pool. If the length of your pool is 8 feet or less, use a board that extends the length of the pool and a smaller (3- to 4-foot) piece of 2 by 4 across the width. Take a reading on diagonals from the edge of the pool to the center where the two boards cross. Take level readings at frequent points around the pool, removing soil from the high spots until the edge is even all around. For a square or rectangular pool, use a short board angled across the corners to make sure the ends are not higher than the sides.

If the pool is so large that a single 2 by 4 will not extend across at its widest dimension, drive a stake in the center of the hole. Place one end of the 2 by 4 on top of the stake and set the other end on the edge of the pool. Place

a level on top of the 2 by 4. Adjust the stake up or down until the 2 by 4 is level with the edge of the pool at that point. Having established the horizontal in one place, use the stake as a pivot point while you move the far end of the 2 by 4 around the pool's perimeter. At each point add or remove soil until the edge is level with the top of the stake. Then remove the stake from the center.

Step 5: Line the excavation with damp sand No matter what kind of soil you have, line the entire excavation with about 2 inches of damp sand as an added cushion. That extra layer of sand helps to smooth out irregularities in the foundation and prevents punctures especially from heaving soil and rocks in cold winters. About ¼ of a ton of sand is sufficient for a pool that has 40 square feet of surface.

Dampen the sand and spread it first on the bottom of the pool. Pack it along the sides, filling in holes and cushioning rocks. Then smooth it with a sheet of thick cardboard or a 2 by 4. Double-check to make sure there are no sharp objects, such as roots, sticks, stones, or rubble, poking through the sand or hidden just beneath the surface. If you find any rough spots, remove the object, then cover the area, and pack it smooth with sand again. When you are done, the walls and bottom should be quite smooth, with no sharp dips or bumps.

Smoothing the Liner

The flexible liner will bunch up at curves and corners. To keep it smooth and neat, fold the liner into neat pleats where it tends to bunch; this is easiest to accomplish with two people.

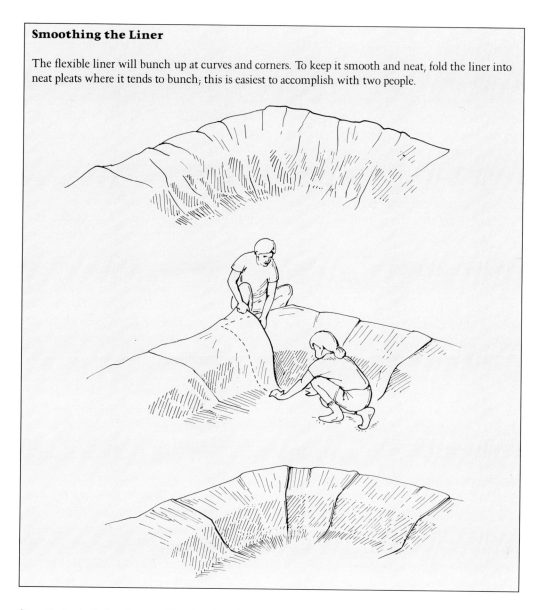

Step 6: Install the liner   The flexible liner should lie flat against the sides and bottom of the excavation, with as few wrinkles or folds as possible. PVC is easier to work with when it is warm and most flexible. Leave the liner in the sun for a while, and it will become more pliable, but don't spread it on a sunny lawn or the grass underneath will be cooked. For a large pond you will need an assistant to help fit the liner and adjust the folds.

Begin by centering the PVC liner over the excavation site. Take off your shoes, get into the pool, and begin pushing the liner outward from the center into the corners. It helps if you have two people for this. As one pushes the liner, the other adjusts the edges, pleating and folding the liner along the sides to fit it into the corners and curves as neatly as possible.

As you work, you may need to readjust the liner to make sure it is still centered in the hole. Like a bedsheet, the overlap at the top edges should be even all the way around. Then fill the liner with 2 inches of water. Smooth out folds and wrinkles before filling.

Continue to fill the pool, stopping at intervals to gather any wrinkles into neat folds. A pool with curved sides will have some folds in all curved areas, but these will go unnoticed when the pool is finished. In a rectangular pool, gather the liner at the corners and pleat it to make neat folds.

When the liner is filled, check for low spots around the top edge. If water is spilling out at any point, lift the liner at that point and build up the soil underneath. When you are finished, water should cover the liner evenly all the way to the top on all sides.

Step 7: Add edging or coping   There should be at least 6 inches of extra PVC showing all around the edge of the pool. To secure and hide the excess liner, dig a shallow trench, place the overlapping PVC in the trench, then cover it with soil, stones, or paving material. If you are laying flat paving around the edge of the pond, the stones should jut out about 2 inches over the water's edge to help hide and protect the liner. (For further details on paving and landscaping around the perimeter, see the chapter "Landscaping Your Garden Pool.")

INSTALLING A PREFABRICATED POOL

The most durable prefabricated pools are made of rigid fiberglass, a very strong material that is almost impossible to puncture accidentally. Exposure to air and sunlight causes discoloration, but does not shorten the life of the material. However, edges exposed above the waterline may become unsightly. Some crazing occurs in fiberglass pools that are allowed to stand empty.

Pools made of other materials, such as bonded resin and semirigid or ABS plastic, are also available. They are less expensive than fiberglass and more fragile. If you choose to use them, follow the instructions for installing fiberglass, but take greater care: Make certain they are well supported with soil or sand, because semirigid pools may change shape, sag, or crack when filled with water if they are not adequately supported on all sides.

Steps for Installing a Prefabricated Pool

There are seven steps to the installation of a prefabricated pool.
1. Select the prefabricated shell.
2. Measure and outline the excavation.
3. Excavate the site.
4. Line the bottom with sand.
5. Level the bottom.
6. Install and fill the shell and backfill around the sides with soil.
7. Add edging or coping.

Step 1: Select the prefabricated shell   Before you buy or order a prefabricated pool, you may wish to lay out an outline in much the same manner as described in step 1 for installing a flexible liner. Use the dimensions given in the supply catalog or obtained from your garden center to try out different shapes and sizes before you buy. Thus you can be sure that the pool will work where you have chosen to place it.

Step 2: Measure for excavation   For an irregularly shaped pond, you will want to have the shell on site to measure for the excavation. If you have ordered a rectangular or circular pond and you know the dimensions, you can measure the site and begin excavating before the shell is delivered.

To mark the excavation, place the shell upright on the site and outline its bottom edge with a heavy rope or hose. Increase the dimensions by 2 inches in every direction and then stake the rope in place.

Step 3: Excavate the site   The excavation should be 2 inches deeper and 2 inches wider than the shell to allow for a layer of sand on the bottom and backfill around the edges. When digging, follow the contours of the shell. You may have to take some measurements as you go along. If the prefabricated pond has built-in marginal shelves, you should leave ledges of soil in the excavation to support the shelves. (In a prefabricated pool, the shell will be weak wherever it is not supported by soil. Semirigid liners, especially, need to be supported at every point to carry the water's weight.)

If you are installing the pool on a grade, you can either excavate the uphill side of the grade or build up the soil as a retaining wall on the downhill side. In building a retaining wall, it is essential that you compact the soil thoroughly to reduce settling. A retaining wall can also be built from brick, stone, or treated railroad ties. Whatever material you use, make sure that the top edge of the pool is level all the way around. And be sure the marginal shelves are supported at all points.

Step 4: Line with sand   When you reach the proper depth and width, scrape and level the bottom, removing all large stones, roots, and rubble. Spread 2 inches of damp sand evenly across the bottom.

Installing a Prefabricated Pool

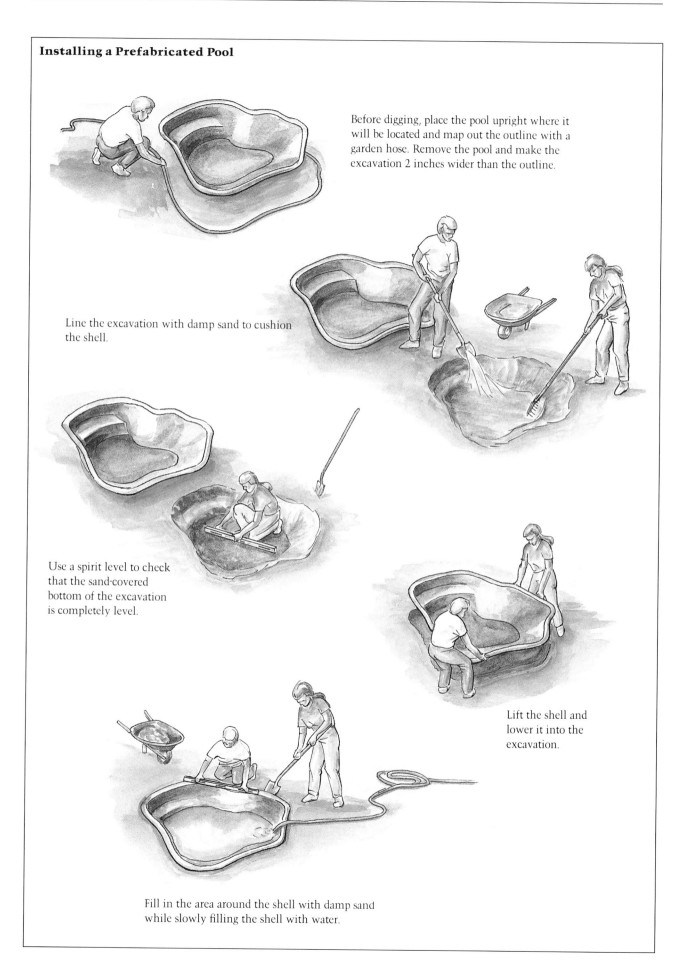

Before digging, place the pool upright where it will be located and map out the outline with a garden hose. Remove the pool and make the excavation 2 inches wider than the outline.

Line the excavation with damp sand to cushion the shell.

Use a spirit level to check that the sand-covered bottom of the excavation is completely level.

Lift the shell and lower it into the excavation.

Fill in the area around the shell with damp sand while slowly filling the shell with water.

Step 5: Level the bottom   The ground underneath the pool must be perfectly level so that the top edges of the pool will be level. Use a 2 by 4 or a piece of heavy cardboard to smooth out the sand on the bottom. With a 4-foot spirit level, check the sand for evenness. If you have only a small level, place it on top of a 4-foot-long 2 by 4 laid on the sand.

Then set the shell in place. For a large pool you will need an assistant to help move the shell in and out of the excavation because it is awkward to handle. Check again to make sure that the top edges are level from side to side and across the diagonals.

If you find that the edges are not even, remove the shell, level the sand bed once again, and replace the shell. You may have to repeat this procedure several times. Patience is strongly advised: It is much easier to make adjustments while the shell is empty. With an inch or two of water in the bottom, it becomes impossible to move. If you fill the shell prematurely and then find it is not level, you will have to drain it and start over again.

Step 6: Fill the pool with water and backfill with soil   Once the shell is in place, begin filling the pond in small increments. Do it gradually because the weight of the water causes the shell to bulge outward slightly. You need to backfill with soil as the water level rises. By tamping down soil around the shell's walls, you make sure that the outside fill supports the sides of the pool at all points.

Begin with about 4 inches of water, then backfill with loose soil and sand between the outside of the pool and the walls of the excavation. Compact the backfill by tamping it down with the edge of a digging bar. Add another 4 inches of water to the pool, backfill again, and repeat the procedure until the pool is filled to the rim and thoroughly supported.

Step 7: Add coping or edging   When the shell is in place and filled, conceal the edges with soil, rocks, or masonry. If the pool only has a small lip or none at all, grass or low-growing plants can be planted up to the edge of the liner to conceal it. Flagstones or paving stones should overhang the edge of the pool by about 2 inches if possible. (See the chapter "Landscaping Your Garden Pool," for details.)

If you are using a pool that has a border of rocklike shapes molded into the design, edge it with plants to make the synthetic material less conspicuous. Or, better yet, place real rocks or masonry directly on the molded lip.

WATER TREATMENT

A garden pool can be filled with tap water from the garden hose, but the water may contain chemicals such as chlorine and chlorine compounds that can be harmful or deadly to fish. Ordinary chlorine in the concentrations used in tap water won't harm plants, but chlorine compounds will. (Ask your local water authority what chemicals are used in the water.) After the pool is filled, you may need to dissipate the chlorine or chlorine compounds. If the water supply contains only chlorine and not the chlorine compounds chloramine or chlorine dioxide, you can simply allow the water to stand for 24 to 48 hours before introducing fish. This allows the chlorine to evaporate.

To counteract chloramine or chlorine dioxide, use a specific agent such as DeChlor®, Novaqua®, or AquaSafe®, which can be purchased from a supplier specializing in fish or water gardening. Follow directions on the label. Usually, fish can be introduced to the pool shortly after the dechlorinating agent has been used. If your water supply contains chlorine compounds, you must treat it even when topping up the pool.

POOL ECOLOGY

In a self-contained garden pool, just as in a natural pool, there is a balanced relationship between plant and animal life. Plant life includes not only aquatic or bog plants that you plant in a pond, but also invited and uninvited algae. Some filamentous algae are desirable—they make a mosslike coat on the surface of the pool liner that gives it a natural appearance. Single-celled algae float in the water and, if other elements are not in balance, can cover a pond with a greenish or brownish colored scum. Fish do feed on algae and benefit from the oxygen the algae give off, but a scummy pool looks unattractive.

In a pool where aquatic plants and fish are properly balanced, algae remain under control, the water takes on a clear greenish color, and you should be able to see your hand when you hold it about 6 inches under the water.

This pool was recently drained and cleaned, causing the pea-soup effect of the water. In a few weeks, when the natural ecology of the pool is reestablished, the water will clear.

After Installation

When your pool is new, you may be concerned about its unnatural appearance. You can see all the plumbing and pumps, and the liner looks unnatural. Soon, however, the water begins to resemble pea soup and you may be even more alarmed. Do not worry—this cloudy water is to be expected in a newly planted pool. Once the pool's aquatic plants and fish become established, the single-celled algae causing the pea soup will die and desirable filamentous algae will camouflage the pool's liner. (See pages 99 to 100 for more about ecological balance.) After a few weeks, the new pool will begin to flourish and look more natural.

Concrete Pool Construction Pointers

When a concrete pool is properly installed, it is a permanent structure that can outlast pools made of any of the lighter materials. If the concrete is poorly mixed or not adequately reinforced, the pool will crack when the soil around it settles or freezes. For this reason you may prefer to consult a professional contractor rather than attempt to install a concrete pool yourself, especially if you have not previously worked with concrete.

In cold climates the excavation must be deep and wide enough to allow for a foundation layer of loose pebbles, gravel, or rubble. In warm climates, if the soil is firm, the foundation layer is not necessary. In cold climates the concrete walls should be at least 6 inches thick to avoid the heaving and cracking caused by shifting, freezing soil. In warm climates concrete 4 inches thick will suffice. To ensure a long life, the concrete should be reinforced through the middle with a framework made from ¾-inch reinforcement rod (number 3 rebar) fastened with twists of steel to create a 12-inch grid.

The walls of the pool must be angled at least 20 degrees from the vertical to prevent the concrete from puddling at the bottom when it is poured. Around the outside edge pour a small lip of concrete (about 3 inches wide), so that the pool is recessed into the topsoil.

The concrete should consist of 1 part cement, to 2 parts sand, and 3 parts ballast (or aggregate), all measured by volume. When the dry ingredients are thoroughly combined, add water until the mixture reaches the right consistency for pouring and molding. No forms are necessary if the concrete is thick enough and if the walls slope gently.

Apply the concrete in a single layer, working the mixture first behind the reinforcing framework and then building it up to cover the wire. After smoothing the surface, allow the concrete to set slowly; the time it takes will depend on temperature and humidity. Once the concrete is set, apply two sealant coats of waterproofing cement; premixed products such as Thoroseal® are easy to use. Follow the manufacturer's directions.

For best results concrete should be poured all in one day, ideally in cool, cloudy weather (but not in rain). If the work has to be done on a hot, dry day, cover the poured concrete with opaque plastic sheeting to prevent its drying out too fast.

The pool can be filled as soon as the surface feels hard and dry. Let the water stand for at least a day and then check the level. If the water level falls noticeably, drain the pool and check for cracks. You may be able to patch the crack with a paint-on sealant or a concrete patching compound such as Fastplug®. A properly built pool should never crack.

In a newly constructed pool, lime from fresh concrete will leach into the water. After the concrete has cured and the pool is filled, let the water stand for a week and then drain it. Next, scrub down the concrete with undiluted vinegar or with muriactic acid mixed with water (10 parts water to 1 part acid) to neutralize the pH. (Follow label cautions.) The acid also etches the concrete and gives it a more weathered appearance.

Concrete may be painted black to give an illusion of greater depth. Mix powdered concrete color additive into the sealant coat according to manufacturer's directions.

FOUNTAINS AND WATERFALLS

Above: The combination of the gargoyle fountain and a low waterfall enhances the straight lines of this formal pool located in a town house courtyard. Below: These three fountains are correctly scaled: Their spray is less than half the width of the pool. This arrangement prevents water from splashing outside the pool, eventually pumping the pool dry.

Flowing water adds movement and sound to a normally quiet landscape. It speaks in different tones, depending on whether it is splashing vigorously, bubbling rhythmically, or lapping gently on rocks and pebbles. If the shape, dimensions, and setting of a pond create the mood of a garden, the addition of moving water augments that mood, making it more expressive, and adding the pleasure of sound to the joy of sight.

Apart from the aesthetic rewards, a fountain or waterfall offers practical benefits. Water sprayed in the air is aerated, which benefits fish. Pumped and recycled water, when filtered, is cleaned of suspended matter and, therefore, is clearer.

Whether you choose a fountain, a waterfall, or both for your garden, you should first consider the effects of moving water on plants. Water lilies will not tolerate being splashed by water or jostled by strong currents. Underwater pool currents must be slight enough that they will not disturb the surface. Aquatic plants with floating flowers and leaves must be out of the range of splashing water. Water lily leaves will rot if continually splashed. Moving water also retards the plants' growth and they will not thrive in it.

The style of a fountain or waterfall should fit the appearance of your garden. An elaborate pool ornament spouting water into a scalloped basin would be completely out of place in an informal pond and a naturalistic landscape. A better choice would be a tiered waterfall flowing over a rocky outcrop. In a formal pool, a stream of water spilling over a straight ledge or shooting from a pottery urn works well. Whatever the style of your garden, the fountain ornament or spray should create an effect that harmonizes with the landscape style.

Choosing a Fountain

Fountains can be of several types. The water may gurgle, springlike, from a pipe with an outlet at the surface or fall from a pipe standing well above the surface. If the pipe is fitted with a nozzle, the water will spray out, rather than fall in a bubbling column. Depending upon the nozzle, the water may flow out in a symmetrical bubble, a tall jet, or, if the nozzle rotates, as a zigzag spray. The pipe may be fitted into an ornamental statue such as a lead or ceramic duck, swan, or frog.

When selecting a fountain, consider its size and the height of its spray in relation to the pool dimensions. A small pool would be overwhelmed by a spray that soars up high and falls back all the way to the water's edge. When a breeze comes up, the spray will be blown beyond the edges of the pond and dissipated; the pond may even be pumped dry. Water splashing onto a nearby patio also looks sloppy. As a rule, the spray should be no taller than half the diameter or width of the pool.

For a very small informal pond, select a simply designed bubbling fountain without statuary. You may choose to have water spilling from a pipe emerging from a rockery

above the pool. In a formal setting, have the water spill from a pipe or statue into a dish or urn, overflow, and then splash down into the pool. Or, line up several nozzled fountains down the middle of the pool. A submerged pump directly underneath a fountain will circulate pool water, creating only a slight current that does not disturb plants or fish except in its immediate vicinity.

Choosing a Pump

To feed a high fountain or waterfall, a pump must generate enough pressure to force water to the discharge point. (The maximum distance that a given pump can send water is called the head. Specifications for some pumps may refer to the pump's maximum head.) Pumps are available in many different

It takes a powerful pump to generate enough pressure for this gushing fountain. The size of pump that a fountain requires depends upon the volume of water to be pumped, the distance the water must travel from the pump, and the height the water will reach.

Spray Types

Fountain sprays come in various types and heights depending upon the size and design of the nozzle. You can change the spray type by selecting a different nozzle.

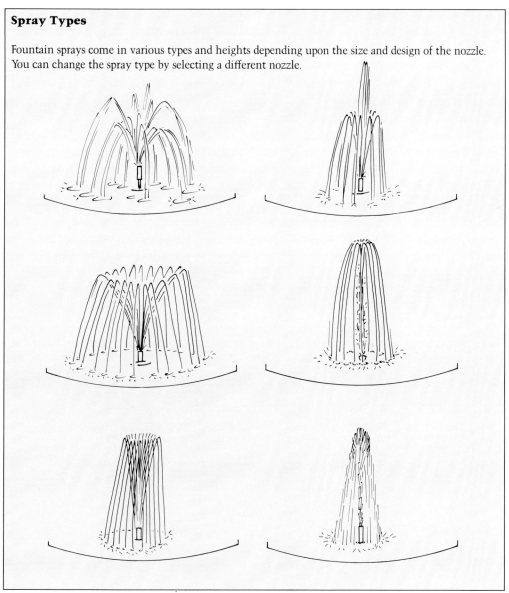

sizes and capacities, so you will have to make some rough calculations to find out which size you need.

In packaging and advertising, the pump manufacturer usually describes maximum theoretical performance; in practice the pump may not be as powerful. Consult a garden center or supplier before ordering and check the performance chart that comes with the pump. Most mail-order catalogs provide this information. Some suppliers will conditionally agree to exchange a pump that turns out to be too small for your pool.

When choosing a pump, you need to find out how many gallons per hour it will pump to the discharge height of the fountain or outlet at the top of a waterfall. The higher the water has to go, the smaller the volume of water that the pump can move. For instance, a pump that circulates 350 gallons per hour to a height of 2 feet may recirculate only 150 gallons per hour to a height of 5 feet.

You also have to consider the distance that the water will be pumped. In general, every 10 horizontal feet of piping reduces the pump's performance as much as 1 foot of vertical piping would. A pump with a maximum head of 4 feet will only reach a 3-foot head if it has to propel the same amount of water through 10 extra feet of piping. Narrow piping creates more friction than does wide piping. For a fountain or a waterfall, choose piping with a diameter that fits directly onto the discharge outlet of the pump. The diameter will vary depending upon the pump's capacity.

Buy a pump that is more powerful than you think you will need; you can always slow it down, but you can't make a weak pump work harder. The rate of flow per hour should not be any greater than the volume of the pool. The pump should circulate at least half the volume of the pool every hour.

Calculating Performance

To calculate the volume of your pool, multiply the length by the width and height (in inches) to give you the number of cubic inches. Then divide by 231, the number of cubic inches in a gallon of water. This tells you how many gallons are contained in the pool. For a pool measuring 72 inches by 104 inches by 18 inches, the calculations would look like this:

$72 \times 104 \times 18 = 134{,}784$ cubic inches
$134{,}784 \div 231 = 583.5$ gallons

To be able to recirculate half of the water in the pool in one hour, the pump should have a rated capacity of about 300 gallons per hour. However, pumps with capacities ranging from 150 to 200 gallons per hour would be adequate.

Installing a Pump

Two types of pump are available, submersible pumps and surface pumps. A surface pump is situated outside the pool in a separate compartment or housing. Because it requires careful installation, it is rarely used in home garden pools. A submersible pump is situated in the pond, is completely submerged and never has to be taken out except when the filter pad needs rinsing. It draws water through a

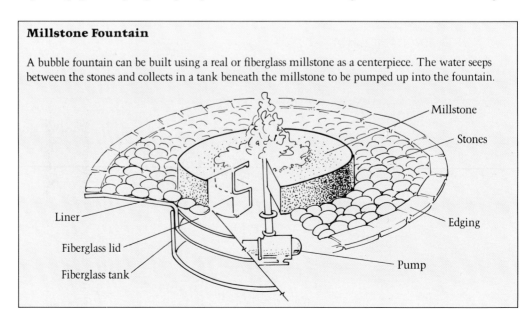

Millstone Fountain

A bubble fountain can be built using a real or fiberglass millstone as a centerpiece. The water seeps between the stones and collects in a tank beneath the millstone to be pumped up into the fountain.

Millstone

Stones

Edging

Pump

Liner

Fiberglass lid

Fiberglass tank

submerged inlet, then drives it through an outlet, called a volute, into a fountain connection or tubing. It does not need priming and, because it is underwater, it is quiet.

Most submersible pumps use regular house current (110 volts), although some smaller pumps need only a low, 24-volt power supply. For low-voltage pumps, a transformer that can be plugged into an outlet comes with the pump. As with all outdoor appliances, it is advisable to install a Ground Fault Circuit Interrupter (GFCI) that will interrupt the electricity if the cord is accidentally cut or frayed. A built-in GFCI must conform to local ordinances and usually should be installed by a licensed electrician. A licensed electrician can also install an outlet near the pool if the cable attached to the pump is not long enough to reach the house. All electrical connections in a submersible pump are sealed tightly, so there is little danger of electric shock. Be sure that any electrical installations conform to your local ordinances.

Since cables, pipes, and fittings are unsightly, they should be covered with soil, turf, or paving. Cables and tubing may be enclosed in PVC piping and buried 18 inches deep to prevent them from being pinched or crushed. They are then difficult to reach without tearing up the landscape. To make a permanent installation, plan carefully and check that all fittings and joints are secure before covering up the piping.

Water Filters

Water filters may be attached directly to the pump's water intake. The filter will keep the water clearer and fresher by reducing suspended algae, and eliminating debris. A simple mechanical filter, consisting of a plastic canister wrapped with a filter pad, is adequate for most garden pools. The only maintenance required is the regular rinsing or replacement of the filter. Biological filters are much more complex and take up more space. Some may require a separate pool up to a quarter the size of the pond itself.

Where to Place a Pump

It's best to place the pump near the base of a waterfall or fountain, rather than at the opposite side of the pond. To minimize the distance from pump to head, reduce the amount of tubing that has to be installed, and increase the force of the fountain. If you are also filtering the water, you'll get the best results if the intake and discharge pipes are at opposite sides of the pool. Whatever arrangement you choose will work well if your pump is sufficiently powerful.

A submersible pump should not be placed directly on the bottom of the pool, since silt, sediment, and leaves on the bottom can clog the intake. Raise the pump with bricks or rocks so the intake screen is at least 2 inches above the floor of the pool, and make sure the pump has a stable base.

Pump Location

Locate the pump that operates a waterfall or fountain as close to the base of the falls as possible.

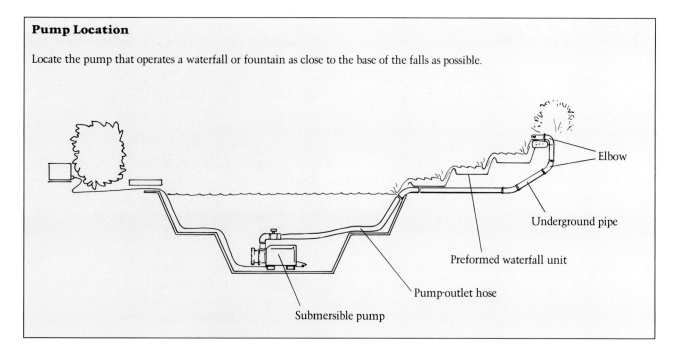

Elbow

Underground pipe

Preformed waterfall unit

Pump-outlet hose

Submersible pump

If you find that the filter intake screen is frequently clogged with large pieces of debris, place the pump inside a submerged container, such as a plastic laundry basket, filled with coarse gravel. The gravel filters out debris before it can reach the pump intake, without measurably slowing down the water's flow.

Since a submersible pump is always surrounded by water, you can start it up at any time without priming. It would run dry only if a large leak or excessive evaporation depleted the pool dramatically. You can shut off the pump and filter if you expect to be away, but if you have fish in the pool, it's best to leave it running. Ask a neighbor to check the pool's water level regularly.

All piping that leads to and from a pump should be of a sturdy material such as heavy-duty PVC or reinforced rubber that will not be compressed by suction or crushed by the weight of soil or water. If you use a flexible discharge tube, be sure not to place heavy containers or rocks on top of it. Pump suppliers and water garden catalogs offer a variety of tubing, valves, connectors, and strainers. It makes sense to purchase good quality fittings to ensure that maintenance and replacement costs are kept to a minimum.

HOW TO BUILD A WATERFALL AND STREAM

Whether it is a trickling, meandering rivulet or a bountiful, splashing cascade, a waterfall or stream provides an expressive, dynamic display. Even if your garden lacks a natural grade, you can build a slope for a waterfall out of the soil excavated from the pool. For a large slope, cover a mound of well-compacted rubble with a layer of topsoil. If made large enough and planned with care, the mound looks natural, adding interest to a flat landscape. Avoid sharp mounds of rock or soil, which look artificial. A gentle slope with outcroppings of rock will seem most realistic and also provide an attractive setting for a rock garden. On a natural grade, the possibilities are infinite, so take advantage of the opportunity to be creative. If you need inspiration, visit public and private gardens and see how falls and flowing water fit into the landscape.

When designing your falls, keep in mind that considerable quantities of water can be lost if allowed to splash outside of the water

channel. To avoid excessive water loss, falls should not splash outside the pool. Unless you plan to purchase a very large pump, the head of the waterfall should not be too far above the surface of the pool. A pool of moderate size will provide enough water to feed an informal waterfall with a head at a level of 2 or 3 feet. Five or six falls can occur over a distance of a few yards. Any waterfall higher than 3 feet should be reserved for a very large pond, and it will require a pump with considerably increased capacity to circulate the greater volume of water. The gain in effect, therefore, must be measured against the additional cost and maintenance of a larger pump.

Waterfall and Stream Materials

Like a pool, a waterfall or stream must be lined with a leakproof material to contain the water and prevent seepage. Though concrete is a possibility, PVC is the recommended material for a liner because it is flexible and, therefore, you can build a waterfall of any design. By concealing the PVC beneath stones

This clever arrangement of smaller rocks around a basinlike rock allows a naturalistic waterfall to be built where there is no natural slope.

and rocks, you can create a completely natural-looking watercourse. When the waterfall is finished, the edges of the PVC can be concealed by rocks, soil, and plants so that the landscape around the channel also looks completely natural. Smooth stones, pebbles, and rocks will camouflage the bottom of the stream and falls and enhance the musical quality of the flowing water.

A number of prefabricated waterfall or stream designs can easily be installed on a natural or man-made grade. Surrounded with ferns and flowers, these units can be very attractive. Most prefabricated fiberglass or plastic waterfalls consist of several tiers in a single unit. You can also purchase separate catch basins made of plastic or fiberglass that can be arranged in a variety of positions. If you are using any of the preformed units, it is especially important to make a level excavation, filling in with sand if necessary. Each unit should be perfectly level. Mounted on the side of a grade, a basin that is out of plumb looks as lopsided and unsightly as a tilted painting.

Since fiberglass and many plastics deteriorate in sunlight, they should not be allowed to go dry unless completely covered with rocks or gravel. If possible, the basins should be tilted slightly backward so that even when the pump is not running they are always filled with water, which will protect the liner and look attractive.

Creating A Naturalistic Effect

You can create different effects by altering the size of a PVC-lined watercourse. Since water flows more rapidly through a narrow channel, you can create a fast-flowing stream with falls by bringing the banks closer together. Or you can make a broad, slowly moving current by widening the channel. Add interest by charting a meandering course and by varying the size and dimensions of each fall. Avoid a long stretch of smooth, shallow water, since slime can build up where the current is too leisurely. For growing special plants, you may want to build some deeper catch basins that can be planted with marginal and bog plants.

Before you dig the water channel, enclose the flexible tubing leading from the pool pump to the head of the waterfall in a rigid PVC conduit and bury it. Or run the water

directly through the protective pipe. The outlet can feed into a small pond at the head of the falls, or it can spout directly into a flowing stream. In either case, conceal the mouth of the pipe with plants, soil, or stones. The most natural effect is produced by water bubbling up through a pipe hidden by a large rock.

Excavate the water channel with a spade and trowel, then cut the PVC to fit. The liner creates a holding area for the rocks, plants, and soil that are in and around the watercourse, so the basin covered by the liner may be much deeper and wider than the final

Above: Taking advantage of the existing grade, this waterfall looks perfect among the naturalistic rock outcroppings. Stones in the watercourse add to the music of the water.
Below: Overhanging plants and rocks conceal the PVC liner that makes this waterfall leakproof.

channel. In measuring the liner, allow for the width of the waterfall and the heights of both banks. Then add at least 6 inches so that the PVC can overlap the surrounding soil and the main pool. Line a small waterfall with a single sheet of PVC, allowing an extra pleat at every drop-off, so you have extra material to cover the sides.

If you are lining a long watercourse and must use several sheets of liner, overlap the separate pieces at each fall. The liner does not need to be sealed at these points, but the upper layer of PVC should generously overlap the lower piece. In each basin, the upper edge of the bottom piece of liner should be above the height of the water, so that there will not be any seepage into the surrounding soil.

Once the liner is in place, trim the excess and bury the edges in trenches covered with soil. Then add rocks, stones, and plants. You can set stones right in the stream, but use only smoothly rounded stones directly on the liner; set rough-edged stones on a layer of pebbles.

Turn on the pump and experiment by moving the stones around to alter the channel and the speed of flow. Stones placed randomly in the center of a stream create rapids. Large pebbles scattered across a shallow bed of water produce ripples. You can make the water break, splash, and tumble by arranging odd-sized stones and pebbles above and below the edge of the stream and falls. If you rearrange the stones at the edge of the fall, you will notice changes in the sound of water as well as in its appearance. The space beneath the falls creates a hollow chamber that projects the echo of falling water.

For a sheetlike effect, extend a flat stone over the edge of the waterfall (see the illustration on opposite page). Water that runs over this flat edge will fall in a clear, vertical plane to the pool below.

A Formal Waterfall

When building a waterfall to feed a traditional pool, you can use PVC—camouflaged beneath pebbles, flat stones, bricks or other masonry—as a liner. The falls are usually spaced at regular intervals creating a staircase of falling water that echoes the symmetry of the garden design. The water drops in a straight sheet from one falls to another. The catch basins should be tilted backward

Building a Waterfall

To build a tiered waterfall on sloping ground, first scoop out the basins, slanting them slightly backward so they hold water. Line the excavation with PVC sheeting. Conceal the edges of the PVC beneath smooth stones and rocks; add rocks to the basins if desired.

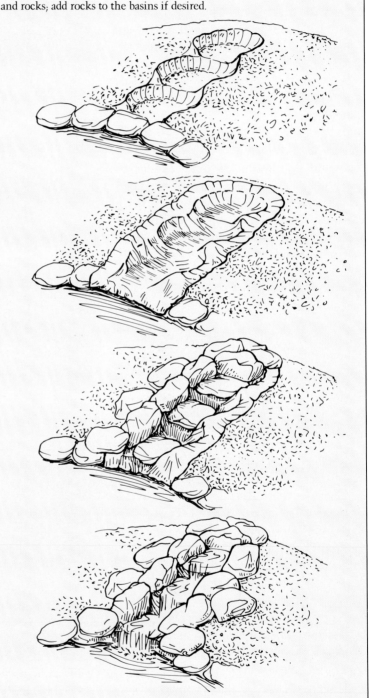

slightly so they hold water when the pump is turned off.

To enhance the symmetry of a formal waterfall, you might extend a piece of a clear Plexiglas sheet or a flagstone beyond the lip of the falls. The water thus moved away from

Improving a Waterfall

Adding stones to the course of a waterfall increases the movement and musical sound of the water. To encourage the water to fall in a translucent sheet, extend beyond the edge of each tier a lip made from a flagstone or a plexiglass sheet.

The huge boulders around this Japanese-style garden account for the realistic appearance of the stream and waterfall.

the wall drops in a translucent sheet that echoes as it tumbles down.

Since any mortar used in construction adds lime to the water, all new surfaces must be thoroughly leached or painted with a sealant before fish and aquatic plants are introduced to the pond (see page 29).

Rocks and Plants Around the Waterfall

The sloping terrain around an informal waterfall is an ideal place for a rock garden. You can simulate a natural stone outcrop with large rocks of mixed sizes partially buried in the soil. In addition to creating a rugged appearance, rocks also serve a practical purpose by preventing erosion along the embankment. Depending upon the climate and the amount of sunlight, you can create a semishaded wildflower and fern garden, a sunny alpine meadow, or a desert garden of succulents and cactus. Around a formal waterfall you can plant an attractive border of flowers or low ground cover backdropped with flowering shrubs and trees.

Planting and Stocking Your Garden Pool

Turn your garden pool into a water garden with aquatic plants and fish.

You may enjoy your garden pool or fountain for the sight and sound of the water alone, but aquatic plants and fish will give it an extra dimension. Nothing is more beautiful on a sunny day than pearly-pink water lily blossoms floating on a quiet pond and goldfish flashing beneath the surface. A water garden provides an opportunity to grow dozens of varieties of plants and fish that thrive in ponds and streams. Avid gardeners often install a garden pool for the express purpose of growing water lilies and other plants that can't be grown in any other environment. Formal pools or unimposing trickle fountains don't require plants, but many gardeners agree that a pool isn't complete without at least one water lily or lotus. In a naturalistic pool, you'll probably want to grow water lilies in the center of the pool and aquatic or bog plants around the edges.

In a garden pool, both plant and animal life benefit from sharing the same habitat. When the pool is well balanced, aquatic plants, desirable kinds of algae, and fish live in harmony. Water-lily leaves spreading across the surface shade the water. This slows algal growth, keeps the water cool for fish, and reduces evaporation. Underwater aquatic plants help control excess algal growth by competing for carbon dioxide and other nutrients in the water, and they benefit fish by giving off oxygen during the day. Fish and algae are interdependent. Fish help to keep the water clear by eating algae. Fish waste, however, fertilizes the algae, stimulating their growth. When the pool is balanced, fish flourish and algae are less likely to get out of control. Fish also limit the mosquito population by feeding on larvae.

Many people install a garden pool for the pleasure of growing aquatic plants. Aquatics in this lush pool include lotus 'Rosea Plena'; hardy water lilies 'William Falconer' (red), 'Flammea' (light red), and 'Marliacea Carnea' (pink); arrowhead; and thalia.

Above: Tropical water lilies, such as this 'Juno', create a dazzling and often highly fragrant display during the hot summer months. Below: Hardy water lilies, such as this 'Rose Arey', over-winter in most climates and begin blooming in the spring when the water has warmed.

WATER LILIES

There are two kinds of water lilies—tropical and hardy, both belonging to the genus *Nymphaea*. Many species and cultivated varieties of both are available from mail-order suppliers. Both will create dazzling color on the surface of your pool, but their care and culture are somewhat different.

Tropical Water Lilies

Tropical water lilies are bred from lilies originating in South America, Africa, Southeast Asia, Australia, and Mexico. They flourish in the summer, holding their shimmering blossoms on tall stems above the water surface. They are profuse bloomers and make exquisite cut flowers. The leaves are round and dark green, maroon, or variegated and, in some varieties, also maroon on the underside.

Tropical water lilies offer a varied palette of color—shades of white, pink, peach, red, yellow, purple, and blue—and are fragrant as well. The tropicals are often many-petalled and most have beautiful centers of yellow stamens. The petals may be sharply pointed, creating a starlike flower, or rounded, creating a cup-shaped blossom. Tropicals produce a profusion of blossoms during hot weather. Each blossom of a day-blooming water lily lasts for three to five days, with the blossoms opening in the morning and closing up in late afternoon. They are sweetly fragrant. Night-blooming water lilies have just the opposite schedule, opening when darkness falls and closing around noon the next day. Many night-blooming varieties are heavily scented.

Some varieties of tropicals are viviparous, producing tiny plantlets in the middle of mature leaves. The plantlets are complete miniatures with tiny leaves, stems, and roots. To propagate the new plants, trim off most of the large pad surrounding the young plant and place it in a 6-inch pot of garden soil, covering the piece of pad with about 1 inch of soil. Place in water 2 inches deep. As the young plant grows, increase the water depth and transplant to a large container.

Hardy Water Lilies

Hardy lilies, bred from wild European and American water lilies, are somewhat less showy than the tropicals, because the blossoms of most varieties aren't as large and they usually float on the water surface rather than stand above it. The distinctive white, pink, yellow, peach, or red blossoms of hardy water lilies add dashes of color to the water garden, and they reappear season after season. Blossoms may be cup-shaped, star-shaped, or double peony–shaped. They do not have the heavy fragrance of many tropical varieties, but may be lightly scented. The round leathery leaves may be dark green or mottled with chestnut-brown. Leaf undersides are sometimes green or purplish. Hardy varieties grow from rhizomes, not tubers, as tropical varieties do.

A few varieties of hardy water lilies start blooming as early as May in Zone 7 and continue until early fall. A single blossom, which lasts three to four days, opens in the early morning and closes by midafternoon each day—a longer blooming period than that offered by most tropicals. Hardy water lilies thrive in cold areas and need not be removed from the pool as long as the water doesn't freeze down to the rootstock. Most hardy water lilies can be grown in Zones 3 to 10.

Some hardy varieties do not bloom well when the temperature exceeds 95° F for prolonged periods. Dark-colored flowers occasionally burn in hot weather. There are no night-blooming hardy water lilies.

Growing Water Lilies

In garden pools, water lilies are usually grown in containers set in the pool. Hardy varieties should be planted in spring after all the ice is off the pond, but you do not need to wait for the last frost date. They may be transplanted as late as a month before the fall frost date. In Zone 6, in mid-Pennsylvania and southern Ohio for instance, hardy lilies may be planted as early as April. Suppliers begin shipping plants to frost-free areas in March.

Tropicals should not be planted until the water has warmed to a steady 70° F at night. In colder water they will go dormant and be difficult to revive. Any water change should be made at least one week before the containers are placed in the pond. In Zone 10, which encompasses southern Florida and Texas, tropicals can survive winters outdoors. In all other zones where frost occurs, the cold kills tropical water lilies unless the tender tubers are stored in a greenhouse pool during the winter, or stored as described on page 104. Most gardeners simply treat tropical lilies as annuals, replacing them every year.

You'll need at least 11 quarts of good topsoil for each plant (see page 43). It would be preferable to use large containers, holding between 14 and 36 quarts, that allow the lilies to grow and multiply for several years before needing division.

When planting, mix a well-balanced garden fertilizer, such as 12-12-12, 5-3-1, or 7-12-5, into the soil at the bottom of the container, so it doesn't leach into the water but does feed the lilies. Use half a cup of fertilizer for each 8 quarts of soil. Also bury a slow-release fertilizer tablet designed for water lilies at the bottom of the container.

Growing Aquatic Plants

Aquatic plants are best confined to containers in order to keep their invasive roots in check. Bog plants need to be barely submerged; if the water is too deep, raise containers on bricks or rest them on marginal shelves. Water lilies and submerged plants can grow in water that is up to several feet deep.

9" deep

18" deep

Bog plant

Tropical water lily

Hardy water lily

Submerged plant

Planting Water Lilies

Plant water lilies in shallow containers of topsoil. Fill the container half full of soil, then position the rootstock. Plant a hardy lily with the main growing point near the edge of the container; center a tropical lily. Add more soil but don't cover the crown. Top off with gravel to prevent soil from clouding the water.

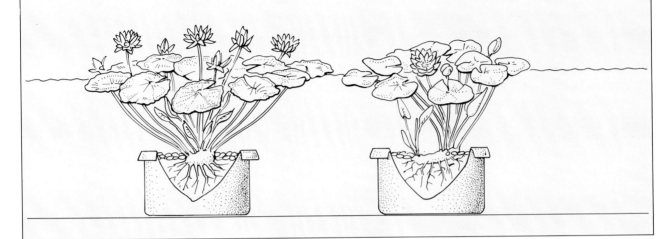

Water lilies need to be fertilized during the growing season. One way to do this is to lift the containers from the pool and press slow-release fertilizer tablets into the soil.

Fill the container halfway full of soil, position the lily, then gently add soil around the roots, leaving the crown uncovered. Tamp the soil down. The rhizome of a hardy water lily grows sideways, so it should be positioned at the edge of the container, with the growing point directed toward the center. Tropical water lily tubers should be centered in the container. Finally, spread a ¼- to ½-inch layer of pea gravel over the top to hold the soil in place and keep it from clouding the water. It is essential that the plant's crown—where the stems meet the roots—be elevated just above the soil and gravel line. (Note the location of the crowns in the illustration above.)

Position the water lily container on cinder blocks in the bottom of the pool, so that the crown is between 6 and 18 inches below the waterline. It will take several weeks for new growth to develop. To speed growth, start by placing the container only 6 inches below the surface, where the water is warm and lit by the sun. Gradually lower the container to its final position as the lily pads grow.

Most water lilies need full sun from ten to twelve hours a day to bloom well. A few varieties, however, will bloom with only three or four hours of sunlight every day, but the more sun they receive, the more flowers they will produce.

Water lilies need to be fertilized regularly. Tropical and hardy lilies should be fed one slow-release fertilizer tablet for every 8 quarts of soil every month during the growing season. Press the tablet in the soil near each plant's roots. You can move small containers to the pool edge to do this, but for lilies in large, heavy containers, it is easier to reach into the pool than to move the containers.

As water lilies grow, their outer leaves may turn yellow. This is normal. Simply remove the unsightly leaves and the water lily will produce new growth. Old blossoms may also be cut off. In fall, after frost, remove the dead foliage from the pool.

As a precaution in winter, lower the containers of hardy lilies to the bottom of the pond before it ices over. If there is any risk of the pond freezing solid, remove the containers before the ice becomes permanent. Allow the soil to drain for a few minutes and trim away all foliage. Wrap the container in moist burlap or peat moss and store, at 40° to 55° F, in a cool corner of the basement or garage. Cover each container with a plastic garbage bag to keep in moisture; check the soil regularly to be sure that it remains moist.

Varieties of Water Lilies

In the charts on the following pages, varieties of hardy and tropical water lilies are grouped according to flower color—white, pink, yellow, blue, purple, and red. In addition three varieties of hardy water lilies, called *changeables* because the color changes from yellow to reddish bronze or apricot as the flowers age, are included. (See opposite page for care and planting.) Tropical water lily varieties are also separated according to whether they bloom in the day or during the night.

Soil and Containers for Aquatic Plants

Water lilies and other aquatic plants are usually grown in submerged containers to prevent them from spreading too aggressively and crowding out less vigorous aquatic plants.

The best containers are plastic because they are strong yet light in weight when compared with other materials. Aquatic plants are shallow-rooted, so generally containers that are wider than they are deep are most suitable. British gardeners use special water lily baskets with woven sides that are lined with burlap before the soil is added; these are not readily available in this country. Instead, you can use heavy-duty dishpans, buckets, clay pots, or special similarly shaped containers sold at garden centers and by mail-order suppliers. Many British authorities recommend that you punch holes in the sides of solid plastic containers to allow for gas exchange, but tests have shown that aquatic plants perform just as well in closed-sided containers.

All aquatic plants need heavy garden soil, preferably containing some clay. Commercial potting mixes designed for houseplants are too light and infertile and will float to the surface. You can fill containers with purchased topsoil or dig it up from your garden. Avoid garden soil that might contain insecticides or herbicides, which may be deadly to the plants and fish in a water garden. Nor should you dig up soil from a boggy area of your property, since it may contain weed seeds that will flourish in your water garden. Aquatic plants will flourish in any of the containers shown here; these are available from aquatic-plant suppliers.

'Comanche'

HARDY WATER LILIES (*Nymphaea*)*

Plant Name	Description	Comments
CHANGEABLE		
'Aurora'	The 2-inch flowers open creamy yellow or yellow-apricot and change to deep red by the third day. Small mottled leaves and compact leaf spread.	Use this pygmy water lily in tub gardens or small pools.
'Comanche'	Flowers are 4 to 5 inches across and held above the water. Open a peachy yellow and mature to a coppery orange. Slightly fragrant. Young leaves are purplish; mature leaves are large, green, and speckled with maroon. Spreads 6 to 12 square feet.	Has the largest flowers of the changeable hardy water lilies. Free-blooming. Use in medium-sized to large pools. Blooms with a minimum of 3 hours of direct sunlight a day.
'Graziella'	Flowers open yellow-apricot and deepen to a rich orange by the third day; measure 2 to 3 inches across. Slight fragrance. Foliage boldly variegated with chestnut.	Useful in a tub garden or a small pool. Blooms with a minimum of 3 hours of direct sunlight a day.
* The dimensions for flower size and leaf spreads given are those to be expected for container-grown plants; plants grown in earth-bottomed ponds will be larger.		

'Firecrest'

'Pink Sensation'

HARDY WATER LILIES (*Nymphaea*)*

Plant Name	Description	Comments
PINK FLOWERED		
'Fabiola'	Blossoms a beautiful clear medium pink with a slight fragrance. Small green leaves. Spreads 4 to 12 square feet.	A prolific bloomer, producing flowers very early and late in the season. Usually several blossoms open at one time. Useful for small ponds because of compact size.
'Firecrest'	Flowers are pink with a hint of lavender and have orange, red, and yellow stamens, creating the effect of fire. Sharp, sweet fragrance. Spreads 6 to 10 square feet.	Moderate bloomer. Use in medium-sized pool.
'Hollandia'	Huge, double flowers are medium pink with deeper pink centers. The blossoms become deeper pink as they age. Slightly fragrant. Spreads 6 to 12 square feet.	An early bloomer. Excellent for cut flowers. A first choice for a medium-sized or large pool.
'Joanne Pring'	Dark pink cup-shaped flowers about 2 inches across. Open pale pink and darken in the center to rich pink. Miniature lily spreading 1 to 6 square feet.	Blooms freely, often with several blossoms open at once. Small leaves and limited leaf spread make this ideal for a tub garden or a small garden pool.
'Marliacea Carnea'	The 3- to 5-inch flowers are pale shell pink and look white from a distance. Outer petals (sepals) and petal bases are distinctly pink. Slightly fragrant. Spreads 1 to 8 square feet.	A prolific bloomer. Suitable for pools of any size. Blooms with 4 hours of direct sunlight. First hardy to break winter dormancy in the West. Named 'Morning Glory' or 'Marliac Flesh' in some catalogs.
'Masaniello'	Resembles 'Somptuosa'. Petals rich pink dotted with red and intensifying in color as the bloom matures. Outer petals (sepals) white. Slightly fragrant. Large blossoms held above water surface. Spreads 6 to 12 square feet.	Use in medium-sized to large pools. Blooms with 4 hours of sunlight, but does better with more.
'Pink Opal'	Flowers deep uniform pink and very fragrant. Bronze-hued leaves. Spreads 3 to 6 square feet.	May bloom only moderately until well established with a colony of several plants.
'Pink Sensation'	Deep clear pink flowers with cream edges measure 6 inches across. Slightly fragrant. Spreads 3 to 6 square feet.	Flowers remain open late into the afternoon. Free-flowering. One of the most admired hardy pinks.
'Rose Arey'	The 8-inch flowers have sharply pointed petals of a rich cerise pink. Very fragrant. Spreads 1 to 6 square feet.	Moderate bloomer until well established in a colony of several plants.
'Somptuosa'	Cup-shaped, 5-inch, double flowers with deep strawberry pink petals. Outer petals (sepals) light pink to white. Slightly fragrant. Spreads 4 to 8 square feet.	A prolific bloomer suitable for pools of any size. Also named 'Sumptuosa' in some catalogs.

* The dimensions for flower size and leaf spreads given are those to be expected for container-grown plants; plants grown in earth-bottomed ponds will be larger.

'Escarboucle'

'James Brydon'

HARDY WATER LILIES (*Nymphaea*)*

Plant Name	Description	Comments
RED FLOWERED		
'Attraction'	Large cup-shaped deep red flowers with white outer petals (sepals). Usually the blossoms open light red on the first day and become a darker red each successive day. Slight fragrance. Spreads 4 to 8 square feet.	Sturdy stems and blossoms make good cut flowers. Excellent for medium-sized and large pools. Blooms with a minimum of 3 hours of direct sunlight a day.
'Escarboucle'	Brilliant red blossoms with pointed petals. Slight fragrance. Spreads 4 to 8 square feet.	Moderate to profuse bloomer. Blossoms stay open late in the day, long after other hardy reds have closed. A top choice for medium-sized and large pools. Plants may be expensive because they are difficult to propagate.
'Gloriosa'	Rich red, 4-inch flowers with pointed petals. Spreads 1 to 4 square feet.	A prolific bloomer. Flowers remain open late in the day. Recommended for tub gardens or small pools. Blooms with a minimum of 3 hours of sunlight a day.
'James Brydon'	Rose red, cup-shaped blossoms 3 to 5 inches across. Delightful fragrance like apples. Leaves bronze-purple to dark green.	Begins blooming about 2 weeks later in spring than most hardies but makes up for this with plentiful blossoms later in the season. Excellent for tub gardens or pools of any size. The best choice for a shaded pool.
'Sirius'	Large star-shaped reddish purple flowers have brilliant orange stamens rather than the usual yellow. Slightly fragrant. Beautiful foliage is green heavily mottled with maroon splotches. Spreads 4 to 8 square feet.	Use in medium-sized or large pools. Blooms with a minimum of 3 hours of direct sunlight a day.
'Splendida'	Outstanding rose red double blossoms. Slightly fragrant. Spreads 4 to 8 square feet.	Flowers with a minimum of 4 hours of sunlight a day. Use in pools of any size.
'Sultan'	Magnificent cherry red, 4- to 8-inch blossoms open pink and darken the second day. Slightly fragrant.	Very free-flowering. Use in pools of any size. Performs well in the deep South, where some hardy red lilies do poorly. Blooms with a minimum of 4 hours of sunlight a day.
'William Falconer'	Cup-shaped, deep red blossoms measure 5 to 6 inches across. May be slightly fragrant. Leaves maroon in spring, changing to green in summer. Spreads 6 to 12 feet.	The deepest red of all hardy water lilies. Useful in small pools.

* *The dimensions for flower size and leaf spreads given are those to be expected for container-grown plants; plants grown in earth-bottomed ponds will be larger.*

'Gonnere'

'Virginia'

HARDY WATER LILIES (*Nymphaea*)*

Plant Name	Description	Comments
WHITE FLOWERED		
'Gladstone'	Large waxy white blossoms with a slight fragrance have especially broad petals. Leaves are green with red-striped stems. Plants spread to cover 4 to 8 square feet.	Leaves are large and the plant spreads extensively; best for large pools. Should be grown in water 1 to 3 feet deep.
'Gonnere'	Blossom is double with more than 65 petals and measures 3 to 4 inches across; resembles a huge floating snowball. Petals are often creased lengthwise, adding to the flower's beauty. Medium-sized leaves. Spreads 3 to 6 square feet or more.	Considered by some people to be the most beautiful white water lily. Blossoms close later in the day than those of most other hardy water lilies. Makes good cut flower. Suited for pools of any size. Named 'Snowball' in some catalogs.
'Marliacea Albida'	Large fragrant blossoms are cup-shaped with narrow petals; the outer petals (actually sepals) are touched with pink. Leaves are average in size and green. Slight fragrance.	An old favorite because it's a reliable amd prolific bloomer usually having several flowers open at once. Use in a medium-sized to large pool.
Nymphaea odorata var. *gigantea*	Very fragrant pure white flowers 6 to 9 inches across. Petals long and narrow. Green leaves. Very wide spreading.	Best for naturalizing in large ponds or lakes as deep as 5 or 6 feet; not recommended for containers in garden pools. A native species and shows much variation in flowers.
'Queen of Whites'	Similar to 'Marliacea Albida' but flowers have more petals and are less cup-shaped. Slightly fragrant. Green leaves have reddish bronze undersides. Spreads 8 to 10 square feet.	Very free-flowering, usually with several blossoms open at one time. Best in medium-sized to large pools.
'Virginalis'	Beautiful cup-shaped flowers with broad waxy petals similar to 'Gladstone', but broader at the petal bases. Flowers and foliage smaller than those of 'Gladstone', but plants are more free-flowering. Spreads to cover 4 to 8 square feet.	Suitable for medium-sized pools, as well as larger ones, because of limited leaf spread. May be grown in water as deep as 3 feet. Has long blooming season; one of earliest to bloom in spring and last to stop blooming in fall.
'Virginia'	Very showy, nearly double flowers reaching about 9 inches across. Spreads 6 to 12 or more square feet.	Blooms for a long season. Blooms with less sunlight than most, needing a minimum of 4 hours direct sunlight each day. Performs best with more sun.

* The dimensions for flower size and leaf spreads given are those to be expected for container-grown plants; plants grown in earth-bottomed ponds will be larger.

'Charlene Strawn'

HARDY WATER LILIES (*Nymphaea*)*

Plant Name	Description	Comments
YELLOW FLOWERED		
'Charlene Strawn'	Star-shaped blossoms of clear medium yellow with center petals darker yellow. Holds blossoms higher above the water than most hardy water lilies. Very fragrant.	Prolific bloomer. Easy to propagate. Opens in late morning and closes in mid-afternoon. Blooms over a long season.
'Marliacea Chromatella'	Cup-shaped creamy yellow flowers measure 2 to 6 inches across. Attractive mottled leaves. Spreads 1 to 8 square feet.	Very free-flowering. Blooms well with 3 hours of direct sunlight. Blossoms stay open later in the afternoon than other hardy water lilies. Use in any size pool. Excellent for tub gardens.
'Pygmaea Helvola'	Small, canary yellow flowers measure 1½ inches across. Leaves are small and lightly mottled. Spreads 1 to 4 square feet.	Blossoms open for only a few hours in the middle of the day. Excellent in a tub garden or small pool. Blooms with 4 hours of direct sun, but performs better with more.
'Sulfurea Grandiflora'	Sulphur yellow star-shaped flowers are fragrant and held slightly above the water surface. Smaller foliage than 'Sunrise'. Spreads 4 to 12 square feet.	Good for small pools. Opens late in the morning and closes early in the afternoon.
'Sunrise'	Showy, rich yellow flowers with narrow curved and somewhat crinkled petals measuring up to 9½ inches across. Slight fragrance. Foliage has reddish brown undersides. Spreads 6 to 12 square feet.	Flowers remain open later in the afternoon than those of most other yellows.

* The dimensions for flower size and leaf spreads given are those to be expected for container-grown plants; plants grown in earth-bottomed ponds will be larger.

'Blue Capensis'

'Blue Beauty'

TROPICAL WATER LILIES (*Nymphaea*)*

Plant Name	Description	Comments
BLUE DAY-BLOOMERS		
'Blue Beauty'	Deep blue or lilac flowers measure up to 8 inches across. Very fragrant. Speckled foliage. Spreads 6 to 8 square feet.	Profuse bloomer. An old reliable water lily and still hard to beat. Can be grown in a tub garden.
'Blue Capensis'	Blue flowers are small to medium in size and held high above the water. Foliage may be speckled. Spreads 6 to 8 square feet.	Prolific bloomer. Does well in shallow water.
'Daubeniana'	A miniature with 2- to 4-inch, light lavender-blue flowers. Fragrant. Foliage may be speckled. Spreads 1 to 3 square feet.	Very free-flowering. Young viviparous plants may bloom while still attached to mother plant. Best tropical for areas of low light. Suitable for a tub garden or small pool.
'Leopardess'	Clear medium blue flowers. Fragrant. Beautiful foliage heavily mottled with deep purple. Spreads 6 to 8 square feet.	Free-blooming. Use in medium-sized or large pools. Blooms with a minimum of 4 hours of direct sunlight a day.
'Mrs. Martin E. Randig'	Rich deep violet-blue with darker outer petals (sepals). Heady fragrance. Leaves have bronze undersides. Spreads 1 to 6 square feet.	Prolific bloomer often with several flowers open at once. Viviparous. Use in tub garden or pool of any size. Blooms with a minimum of 4 hours of direct sunlight a day.
Nymphaea colorata	A pygmy variety with 3- to 4-inch flowers. Petals light violet-blue with pale bases and purple stamens. Very fragrant. Spreads 1 to 6 square feet.	Prolific bloomer. Ideal for a tub or small pool. Blooms with a minimum of 3 hours of direct sunlight a day.
'Pamela'	Very large, sky blue flowers held high above the water. Fragrant. Deep green leaves blotched with purple. Spreads 6 to 12 square feet.	A top performer, blooming for a long season. Combine with 'Director George T. Moore' for an eye-catching color combination in medium-sized to large pools.
'Robert Strawn'	Small to medium-sized lavender-blue blossoms are held high above the water. Fragrant. Foliage may be speckled. Spreads 1 to 8 square feet.	Blooms with a minimum of 4 hours of direct sunlight a day.

* The dimensions for flower size and leaf spreads given are those to be expected for container-grown plants; plants grown in earth-bottomed ponds will be larger.

'Pink Platter'

'Pink Capensis'

'Director George T. Moore'

TROPICAL WATER LILIES (*Nymphaea*)*

Plant Name	Description	Comments
PINK DAY-BLOOMERS		
'Evelyn Randig'	Large, bright magenta, star-shaped flowers with yellow centers. Very fragrant. Beautiful foliage variegated with magenta and chestnut. Spreads 6 to 8 square feet.	Free-flowering. Good in pools of any size.
'General Pershing'	Large, very double, orchid-pink blossoms have pink-tipped yellow stamens. Fragrant. Leaves with distinctive red blotches. Spreads 6 to 8 square feet or more.	Free-flowering. Blossoms open in early morning and close at dusk, appearing over a long season. One of the finest tropicals.
'Pink Capensis'	Medium-sized blossoms of a clear bright pink. Leaves green with some speckles. Fragrant. Spreads 6 to 8 square feet or more.	Good in pools of any size.
'Pink Perfection'	Rose-pink blossoms. Fragrant. Heavily mottled foliage. Spreads 6 to 8 square feet or more.	Blooms with a minimum of 4 hours of direct sunlight a day. Will bloom in pools up to 3 feet deep.
'Pink Platter'	Large, double, clear pink flowers. Golden stamens with pink tips fill the centers of the flat blossoms. Fragrant. Foliage speckled. Spreads 6 to 8 square feet.	Viviparous; may produce plantlets at leaf nodes. Use in pools of any size.
'Pink Star'	Medium pink, star-shaped flowers held high above the water. Fragrant. Large foliage. Spreads 6 to 12 square feet or more.	Best in medium-sized to large pools where large foliage looks at home.
PURPLE DAY-BLOOMERS		
'Director George T. Moore'	Striking deep violet-blue flowers with bright yellow centers and purple stamens. Blossoms measure 6 to 8 inches across. Fragrant. Compact speckled foliage. Spreads 6 to 8 square feet.	Blooms with a minimum of 3 hours of direct sunlight a day. Useful in pools of any size.
'Panama Pacific'	Medium-sized bluish blossoms deepen to rich purple. Bright yellow centers of yellow stamens tipped with purple. Very fragrant. Speckled foliage. Spreads 3 to 8 square feet.	Free-flowering. Suited to pools of any size. Plants are viviparous; late in the season, leaf nodes may produce plantlets that bloom while still attached to the mother plant.

* The dimensions for flower size and leaf spreads given are those to be expected for container-grown plants; plants grown in earth-bottomed ponds will be larger.

'Albert Greenberg'

'Yellow Dazzler'

'White Delight'

TROPICAL WATER LILIES (*Nymphaea*)*

Plant Name	Description	Comments
ROSY YELLOW DAY-BLOOMERS		
'Afterglow'	Yellow-centered blossoms have deep pink petals shading to burnished orange at the edges. Very fragrant.	Free bloomer suited to medium-sized or large pools. Blossoms slightly larger than 'Albert Greenberg'.
'Albert Greenberg'	Cup-shaped blossoms a blend of orange, yellow, and deep pink similar to 'Afterglow'. Fragrant. Foliage heavily mottled. Spreads 6 to 10 square feet.	Robust plant that blooms until frost. Blooms with a minimum of 4 hours of direct sunlight a day.
WHITE DAY-BLOOMERS		
'Marion Strawn'	Large white flowers and speckled foliage. Fragrant. Spreads 4 to 8 square feet.	Vigorous grower and good bloomer for medium-sized to large pools.
'Mrs. George H. Pring'	Striking off-white flowers are held high above the water and measure up to 8 inches across. Very fragrant. Spreads 6 to 12 square feet.	Prolific bloomer. Usually one or more blossoms open at a time. Use in medium-sized to large pools.
'White Delight'	Creamy white blossoms—sometimes with a soft pink tint at the petal tips—are held high above the water. Flowers may measure up to 12 inches across. Very fragrant. Speckled foliage. Spreads 6 to 12 square feet or more.	Large leaves and spread make it suitable for medium-sized to large pools. Blossoms remain open an hour or two later than those of most other tropicals.
YELLOW DAY-BLOOMERS		
'Aviator Pring'	Very large, deep yellow, star-shaped flowers held high above the water. Very fragrant. Mottled foliage with crimped edges.	Free-flowering. Excellent for medium-sized or large pools.
'St. Louis'	Soft lemon yellow, star-shaped flowers measure 6 to 8 inches across. Very fragrant. Foliage speckled. Spreads 6 to 12 square feet.	Prolific bloomer. Needs a minimum of 4 hours of sunlight a day to bloom, but performs better with more.
'Yellow Dazzler'	Rich, bright yellow, double blossoms. Very fragrant. Speckled foliage. Spreads 6 to 10 square feet.	Flowers remain open until dusk. Use in medium-sized to large pools. Strongly resembles 'St. Louis'.

* The dimensions for flower size and leaf spreads given are those to be expected for container-grown plants; plants grown in earth-bottomed ponds will be larger.

'Texas Shell Pink'   'Wood's White Knight'

TROPICAL WATER LILIES (*Nymphaea*)*

Plant Name	Description	Comments
PINK NIGHT-BLOOMERS		
'Mrs. George C. Hitchcock'	Huge light to medium pink blossoms with outer petals (sepals) darker pink. Bronzy maroon foliage. Spreads 6 to 12 square feet. Fragrant.	Free bloomer. Continues blooming late into the season. Provide plenty of room for best growth. Use in medium-sized to large pools.
'Texas Shell Pink'	Huge pale pink blossoms are star-shaped. Spreads 6 to 8 square feet. Fragrant.	Prolific bloomer. The blossoms show up well at night on a dark pool. Use in a medium-sized or large pool.
ROSE-RED NIGHT-BLOOMERS		
'Emily G. Hutchings'	Deep pinkish red flowers. Bronze foliage. Spreads 6 to 8 square feet. Fragrant.	Prolific bloomer often producing clusters of flowers. Requires a minimum of 4 hours of direct sunlight a day to bloom. Use in medium-sized to large pools.
'H. C. Haarstick'	Large flowers with deep pinkish red petals tinged with purple at the bases. Beautiful bronzy purple foliage. Spreads 6 to 8 square feet. Fragrant.	Prolific and reliable bloomer. Use in medium-sized to large pools.
'Red Flare'	Spectacular flowers have long, narrow, deep dusky red petals and maroon stamens. Foliage deep mahogany red. Spreads 6 to 8 square feet. Fragrant.	Very free-flowering. Use in medium-sized to large pools.
WHITE NIGHT-BLOOMERS		
'Juno'	Large pure white flowers and green foliage. Spreads 6 to 8 square feet or more. Fragrant.	Blooms in water as deep as 3 feet and with a minimum of 4 hours of direct sunlight each day. Tends to develop multiple crowns, which produce numerous smaller blossoms. Use in medium-sized to large pools.
'Missouri'	Creamy white flowers up to 12 inches across. Young foliage is coppery brown, maturing to green. Leaves have distinctive fluted edges, which allow water to partially cover the pads. Spreads 8 square feet or more. Fragrant.	Use in medium-sized to large pools.
'Sir Galahad'	Huge pure white blossoms held high above the water. Spreads 8 square feet or more. Fragrant.	More prolific bloomer than 'Missouri'. Use in medium-sized to large pools.
'Wood's White Knight'	Large star-shaped creamy white flowers open flat. Spreads 6 to 8 square feet or more. Fragrant.	Very prolific bloomer. Blooms with a minimum of 4 hours of direct sunlight a day.

* The dimensions for flower size and leaf spreads given are those to be expected for container-grown plants; plants grown in earth-bottomed ponds will be larger.

Nelumbo nucifera 'Speciosa'

LOTUS

Lotus, relatives of the water lily, are famed for their huge blossoms and the musky fragrance that can fill a garden on a warm summer's night. Their flowers are sacred to Buddhists and the plants are also grown in the Orient for their edible tubers.

The spectacular blossoms may rise as much as 5 feet above the water. The round leaves, which can measure 2 to 3 feet across, may lie on the surface of the pond or rise on stems like parasols 3 to 6 feet above the water. Leaf color ranges from deep green to blue-green. Miniature varieties are available and make a good choice for small garden pools or tub gardens.

The exotic lotus has 10-inch blossoms with a haunting aroma. The large buds begin to open, usually in midsummer, when the water has been near 80° F for about two weeks. The flower takes about three days to open fully, opening each morning and closing each afternoon, and lasts for three to four days once fully open. After the petals fall, the yellow, flat-topped center turns green and a cone-shaped seedpod develops. This grows larger, turning brown as it matures. These seedpods are quite ornamental and are prized for dried flower arrangements.

Depending on the variety, lotus are hardy in different zones, as noted in the chart on the following page. It may take a year for a new tuber to become established and the plant may not bloom until the second year. Lotus will spread aggressively and can entirely take over an earth-bottomed pond; plant them in large containers so they have plenty of room but are still confined. Like those of water lilies, the rootstocks of lotus should never be allowed to freeze.

Growing Lotus

Lotus are transplanted as semidormant tubers pulled from the mother plant. They are available from mail-order suppliers only during a short period each year, from May to early June. You can grow lotus in submerged containers in much the same way that water lilies are grown. But they need very large containers; those measuring 3 feet by 3 feet or larger are best. Even pygmy varieties need containers that will hold at least 32 quarts. Place the tuber in heavy soil, covering all but the growing tip with about 1 inch of sand. When handling the tuber, be careful not to touch the growing tip as it is easily damaged. Submerge the containers from 2 to 6 inches below the water surface. Fertilize as for water lilies. (See pages 41 to 43 for detailed instructions on care and planting.) All varieties require at least six hours of direct sunlight for flowering.

Nelumbo lutea

'Empress'

LOTUS (*Nelumbo*)*

Plant Name	Description	Comments
American Lotus (*N. lutea*)	Light yellow blossoms with golden centers and stamens reach 10 inches across. Flowers rise above the foliage to stand 3 to 5 feet above the roots. Circular leaves 1 to 2 feet across.	Hardy in Zones 4 to 9. A native American plant. Use in medium-sized to large pools.
Angel Wings Sacred Lotus (*N. nucifera* 'Angel Wings')	Large, single white blossoms. Very fragrant. Circular deep green leaves, 1 to 2 feet across.	Recent, superior variety. Holds blossoms high above the foliage. Hardy in Zones 5 to 9. Restrained growth. Use in pools of any size.
Empress Sacred Lotus (*N. nucifera* 'Empress')	Beautiful single flower with white petals blushed with rose on the edges. Yellow centers with yellow stamens. Fragrant. Circular leaves deep green, 1 to 2 feet across.	Moderate bloomer. Hardy in Zones 5 to 9. Use in medium-sized to large pools.
Momo Botan (*N. nucifera* 'Momo botan')	Deep pink double blossoms resemble peony flowers and measure about 6 inches across. Smaller than other lotus, with restricted growth and 12- to 18-inch-wide foliage.	Hardy in Zones 5 to 10. Excellent in small to medium-sized pools or tub gardens. The similar variety, 'Momo Botan Minima' has 4- to 12-inch-wide leaves, grows 18 inches tall, and is ideal in a tub garden.
Mrs. Perry D. Slocum (*N. nucifera × lutea* 'Mrs. Perry D. Slocum')	Magnificent double blossoms open deep pink, change to pink and yellow on the second day, and become cream with a touch of pink on the third day. Very fragrant.	Free-flowering. A hybrid between *N. lutea* and *N. nucifera* 'Rosea Plena'. Hardy in Zones 5 to 10. Use in pools of any size.
Rosea Plena (*N. nucifera* 'Rosea Plena')	Huge, double, deep rose pink flowers with yellow centers. Very fragrant.	Very free-flowering. Hardy in Zones 5 to 9. Use in medium-sized to large pools.
Sacred Lotus (*N. nucifera* 'Speciosa')	Beautiful single blossoms with rich pink petals tinted cream at the base. Prominent yellow centers and stamens. Blossoms become lighter in color as they age. Fragrant.	Free-blooming. Use in medium-sized to large pools. Hardy in Zones 5 to 10. Sometimes incorrectly called the "Hindu" or the "Egyptian" lotus, this plant actually originated in India, was taken to Persia and, from there, reached Egypt.
Shirokunshi (*N. nucifera* 'Shirokunshi')	Creamy white, 6- to 8-inch-wide, tulip-shaped flowers. Fragrant. Grows only 18 to 24 inches tall.	Hardy in Zones 5 to 10. Well suited to tubs or small pools. May also be used in medium-sized or large pools.
White Sacred Lotus (*N. nucifera* 'Alba Grandiflora')	Very fragrant, single, white blossoms with large rounded petals and green centers with yellow stamens. Circular leaves deep green, 1 to 2 feet across.	Free-flowering. Foliage may obscure flowers. Hardy in Zones 5 to 9. Use in medium-sized to large pools.

* The dimensions for flower size and leaf spreads given are those to be expected for container-grown plants; plants grown in earth-bottomed ponds will be larger.

'Rosea Plena'

Varieties of Lotus

The varieties listed in the chart were bred from the American lotus, *Nelumbo lutea* and the sacred lotus *N. nucifera*, which are sacred to Buddhists. The Egyptian lotus, which was sacred to the ancient Egyptians, is actually a water lily, *Nymphaea caerulea*.

MARGINAL BOG PLANTS

Besides water lilies and lotus, many other attractive upright and spreading aquatic plants flourish in a garden pond. Those called *marginal* plants grow in the boggy and shallow areas around the edges of a pond.

Grown for their flowers, foliage, or both, the marginal plants described later in this chapter include beautiful irises, elegant dwarf papyrus, delicate water arums, and stately cattails. Some are native American plants, such as the blue flag iris, pickerel rush, and arrowhead. All these plants are adapted to the American climate and are available in this country through mail-order suppliers. You may find many plants described in British garden books not included here. That's because they either don't grow well in North American climates or aren't available.

All marginal plants have roots that grow in soil and leaves that float on the surface of the water or stand upright above it. These aquatics look best with an inch or two of water above their roots, but many don't need any water above them at all, as long as the soil around their roots is wet at all times. Marginal plants prosper in shallow garden pools, in pockets of boggy soil, or in specially prepared bog gardens. You can plant them in containers of soil and set these on shelves inside the edges of your pool. (See page 83 for instructions on building a bog garden.)

Marginal plants include both tropical and hardy plants. Tropicals are suited to year-round culture in warm-winter climates and require special care in cold-winter regions if you intend to replant them the following summer. Hardy plants survive cold winters and many can be grown throughout the country.

Growing Marginal Bog Plants

Marginal aquatic plants can be grown, in heavy soil, in 2-gallon plastic pails or pans placed with their rims 2 to 4 inches below the waterline. Place the container on bricks at first, if necessary, to raise it high enough. You can lower it gradually to the maximum depth given for each particular plant as the plants become taller. Add one fertilizer tablet at planting time, as described for water lilies, and additional tablets when the blooming plants begin to develop flowers.

You may wish to plant several of the same plant in one large container to give a fuller look. Allow for three plants in a 5- to 10-gallon container. The plants may need to be divided every three years. Aggressive growers may need to be divided every year. Though they can look very attractive together, it is best not to mix different types of plants, because the stronger growing will crowd out the weaker.

When bog plants are grown in containers, their invasive roots cannot spread. Although clay pots are not usually recommended because of their weight, they look especially pretty raised just above the water level.

Bog plants can be grown in special bog gardens that are kept constantly wet. Here, Japanese iris grow in half-whiskey barrels where they can be given plenty of water.

The ultimate size a bog plant reaches when grown in a container depends upon the size of the container—large containers encourage growth and spreading; small containers often keep plants smaller than their natural height. In a large water garden where you want tall, dramatic accent plants, be sure to plant in large containers. In a small garden pool, keep marginal plants from overpowering the pool by confining them to small containers.

Most marginal and bog plants are invasive. In a garden pool, they should only be planted in containers that can be removed for root pruning or repotting. Water arum and golden club are exceptions: They remain in clumps that can easily be separated and removed from the pond or bog.

Often, bog plants can be planted in a bog garden made of heavy topsoil that is kept moist by an underlining of PVC (see page 83). You may wish to plant them in a low-lying, naturally boggy area of your garden. However, natural bogs are susceptible to invasive weeds, which will quickly take over the more slow-growing cultivated varieties that you introduce.

Varieties of Hardy Bog Plants

The hardy bog plants described here have adapted to North American growing climates and are readily available from garden centers or mail-order suppliers. Most included here will last through winter in Zones 6 to 10, and some are cold hardy to Zones 3 and 2. The heights given are those that may be expected of container-grown plants; plants in large containers or in earth-bottomed ponds will be larger. The season of bloom varies from early spring to late fall. However, many of these plants are grown exclusively for their distinctive foliage.

Arrowhead *(Sagittaria latifolia)* Arrowhead produces stalks of delicate white, 3-petalled flowers above arrow-shaped leaves from early until late summer. Reaches 2 feet tall. The variety 'Flore Pleno' (*S. japonica* in catalogs) has double flowers. Tubers are edible. This native American plant is hardy in Zones 5 to 10. Plants emerge in spring later than many other marginal plants. Easy to grow, but suffers a severe setback upon transplanting. Plant in containers lest it spread too aggressively. Use in groups along borders or as an accent plant. Needs wet soil; will grow in water up to 6 inches deep. Grow in full sun or partial shade.

Cattails (*Typha* species) Cattails are traditional aquatic plants grown for their strong vertical foliage and fascinating velvety brown catkins. Several species are useful in water gardens. *T. latifolia*, common cattail, grows upright to 7 feet tall. *T. laxmannii*, graceful cattail, has narrow 4-foot long leaves. *T. minima*, dwarf cattail, has spiky foliage to 3 feet tall and plump catkins. *T. angustifolia*, narrow-leaved cattail, has graceful slender leaves reaching 6 feet tall. Common cattail and narrow-leaved cattail are hardy in Zones 2 to 10 and grow in wet soil or in water up to 12 inches deep. Dwarf cattail (Zones 5 to 9) and graceful cattail (Zones 3 to 10) will grow in 6-inch-deep water. All grow in full sun to partial shade and are invasive if not contained. When grown in containers, they will not grow as tall.

Chinese water chestnut (*Eleocharis dulcis*)

Dwarf bamboo (*Dulichium arundinaceum*)

Narrow-leaved cattail (*Typha latifolia*)

Chinese water chestnut *(Eleocharis dulcis)* The graceful stems of the Chinese water chestnut are actually cylindrical leaves. The edible tubers are harvested in fall. They are used in Asian cooking and are the crunchy white vegetable in stir-fried Chinese food. Stems grow upright 1 to 3 feet tall. Produces 1-inch-tall spikes of dense straw-colored flowers from summer to fall. Use in small-scale groups for rushlike accent. Grow in wet soil or in water up to 6 inches deep in full sun or partial shade. May take a while to get established. Hardy in Zones 7 to 10.

Dwarf bamboo *(Dulichium arundinaceum)* Not a true bamboo, this plant produces stalks that reach 1 to 3 feet tall and closely resemble bamboo. The blossoms are small and insignificant. An excellent hardy plant useful as a low screening or border plant in a small or medium-sized pool. Grow in shallow water. Hardy in Zones 6 to 10.

Arrowhead (*Sagittaria latifolia*)

Flowering rush (*Butomus umbellatus*)

Floating-heart (*Nymphoides peltata*)

Golden-club (*Orontium aquaticum*)

Floating-heart *(Nymphoides peltata)*

The pretty yellow flowers of floating-heart dot the water surface from spring through fall. They are held slightly above the heart-shaped, 3-inch-wide, green and maroon variegated leaves. These plants trail across the water surface and the small scale of their foliage makes a pleasing contrast to water lily pads. A prolific grower, floating-heart produces new plants on stolons, much like a strawberry plant. May need to be cut back during the growing season, if it spreads too far. Grow in full sun or partial shade in water 4 to 12 inches deep. Hardy in Zones 6 to 10.

Flowering rush *(Butomus umbellatus)*

The flowering rush produces graceful clusters of 3-petalled, pink flowers and blooms for 2 weeks in summer. The stems of these lovely flowers are triangular in cross section, an oddity in nature. The rushlike foliage grows to 3 feet. Looks best used alone or in a simple grouping of aquatic plants where its unassuming elegance needn't compete with showier plants. Grow in full sun in wet soil or water up to 6 inches deep. Hardy in Zones 6 to 10, though doesn't prosper in many parts of California.

Golden-club *(Orontium aquaticum)*

The deep green leaves of golden-club are covered with a wax so thick that water beads up on them like mercury. Golden-tipped white spikes of tiny flowers rise above clumps of ribbed blue-green leaves in early spring. Clumps up to 1 foot high. Use this native plant as a specimen along the edge of a pool or stream. Withstands cool, slowly moving water. Grow in partial shade. Does best in wet soil or shallow water, but will grow in water up to 6 inches deep. Hardy in Zones 6 to 10.

Horsetail *(Equisetum hyemale)*

Horsetail forms upright clumps of cylindrical leaf-

Horsetail (*Equisetum hyemale*)

Her Highness (*Iris* 'Her Highness')

Blue flag (*Iris versicolor*)

Red iris (*Iris fulva*)

less green stems with a brown stripe at each joint. Stems are tipped with interesting brown cones. Also called scouring rushes, horsetails made themselves useful during colonial times as pot scrubbers because their rough stems contain silica. Use this fascinating plant as a fine-textured vertical accent in the corners of a pool or along a stream. Desirable for its year-round green color in mild climates. Does best in partial sun; does poorly in full sun. Grows prolifically when planted just above the water level where occasional flooding occurs. Withstands cool, moving waters. Hardy in Zones 3 to 9.

Iris (*Iris* species and varieties) Several varieties of iris thrive in water gardens. They are prized for their graceful upright leaves and elegant blossoms. Iris flowers are several inches across and appear in early to late spring. The plants will spread and form large clumps if given enough room.

Irises look dramatic as accent plants in a formal garden pool. They are equally at home in a naturalistic setting or bog garden where they can spread. Iris foliage creates a strong upright effect that is beautiful even without the flowers.

The blue flag (*Iris versicolor*) is an American bog iris, native to the swamps of the northeastern states and Canada. It has many natural color variations, ranging from light blue to deep Wedgwood blue. The 3-foot-tall, sword-shaped leaves are topped by stalks of blossoms for two weeks in early to midspring. Hardy in Zones 4 to 10.

Her highness iris (*Iris* 'Her Highness') offers stately large white flowers in early to late spring. This hybrid iris reaches 2 feet in height. Grow in groups of three or more plants for best effect. Hardy in Zones 7 to 10.

Red iris (*Iris fulva*) is native to swamps in the East and Midwest. It produces small, coppery red blossoms in early to late spring. The

Yellow flag (*Iris pseudacorus*)

Lizard's tail (*Saururus cernuus*)

Marsh marigold (*Caltha palustris*)

narrow leaves are bright green and graceful. Plants range from 8 to 24 inches in height. The red color combines well with the yellows of spring bloomers such as marsh marigold. Hardy in Zones 5 to 10.

Yellow flag (*Iris pseudacorus*) has tall, lance-shaped foliage that can reach 4 feet or more in height. Leaves are topped by large, rich yellow blossoms for two weeks in early spring. Even in full sun, the blossoms hold their color well. Native to Europe and Africa, yellow flag has naturalized in North America. Hardy in Zones 4 to 10.

Plant iris rhizomes in boggy soil along the banks of a water garden or in shallow containers that may be set so that the soil surface is several inches below the waterline. Yellow irises can grow in water 12 inches deep, but the other varieties should be in water no deeper than 6 inches. Irises prefer slightly acid soil with some humus. When planting, clip back all the leaves to a height of several inches so that top-heavy foliage won't pull down the plant before the roots can anchor it. For the best effect, group three plants in a 5-quart or larger pot. After the first season you can propagate the plants by dividing the rhizomes in spring.

The yellow water iris requires full sun, but the other varieties will bloom if they receive a minimum of three hours of direct sunlight, although they may become spindly. To keep the plants looking tidy, clip off the dead blossoms.

Lizard's tail (*Saururus cernuus*) The fragrant small white flowers of lizard's tail

bloom on long, curved spikes during early to midsummer. Foliage is heart-shaped on 18-inch stems and may turn lovely bronze hues in autumn. Grow in full sun or partial shade in wet soil or in water up to 6 inches deep. Hardy in Zones 4 to 10.

Marsh marigold (*Caltha palustris*) A native American bog plant, marsh marigold is one of the first flowers to bloom in spring. For a month or more, clusters of large, shiny blossoms like buttercups make golden mounds above the clumps of round leaves. Clumps grow about 1 foot high. The main disadvantage of this colorful plant is that the foliage dies back by midsummer. Grow on banks or in containers barely covered by water. Combine with other plants to conceal the bare spaces in summer. Hardy in Zones 5 to 7. Double and white forms are available. May be difficult to obtain; purchase from native-plant supplier.

Pickerel rush (*Pontederia cordata*)

Parrot's-feather (*Myriophyllum aquaticum*)

Yellow snowflake (*Nymphoides cristatum*)

Primrose willow (*Ludwigia uruguayensis*)

Parrot's-feather *(Myriophyllum aquaticum)* This fine-textured foliage plant produces whorls of blue-green, needlelike leaves. These float just below the water surface with the stem tips curving upward a few inches above the water. Its feathery growth contrasts beautifully with bolder-textured aquatics. Flowers are insignificant. Use in pools of any size for its fine-textured effect. Plant as groups of cuttings in water 4 to 12 inches deep. May need thinning out to keep within bounds. Hardy in Zones 6 to 10.

Pickerel rush *(Pontederia cordata)* Also called pickerel weed, this native American bog plant adorns water gardens from midsummer to fall with spikes of purple, blue, bluish white, or pure white flowers. The shiny lance-shaped foliage cloaks 2- to 3-foot tall stems. The blue pickerel rush is somewhat showier and establishes itself more quickly than the more commonly available purple and white

varieties. Looks best in mass plantings. Plant in full sun or partial shade. Hardy in Zones 3 to 10. In the North, grow in water 12 inches deep to ensure winter hardiness.

Primrose willow *(Ludwigia uruguayensis,* also *Jussiaea uruguayensis)* Neither a primrose nor a willow, primrose willow gets its name from its willow-shaped leaves and primrose yellow flowers. The stems and foliage can rise from 8 to 18 inches above the water. The 2-inch flowers bloom all summer. Use primrose willow in the back or corners of a large water garden. May be rooted in crevices of rocks and waterfalls. It may become invasive in southern areas; control by regular pruning. Hardy in Zones 7 to 10.

Snowflake *(Nymphoides cristatum* and *Nymphoides geminata)* White snowflake (*N. cristatum*) and yellow snowflake (*N. geminata*) produce tiny fluffy flowers rising

Sweet flag (*Acorus calamus*)

Thalia (*Thalia dealbata*)

just above the floating leaves. White snow-flake has green leaves with chestnut markings; the leaves of yellow snowflake are chocolate-brown with green veins and yellow blotches. Leaves mature at different sizes, varying from about 1 to 4 inches across, and provide an interesting texture. Use in masses in the foreground of pools of any size. Grow in full sun or partial shade in water 6 inches deep. Yellow snowflake may spread aggressively; weed out excess to keep in bounds. Hardy in Zones 6 to 10; white snowflake may be more tender.

Sweet flag *(Acorus calamus)*　The sword-shaped, irislike foliage of the sweet flag gives off a strong sweet aroma when crushed. This very hardy plant may be entirely green or variegated with green and white vertical stripes. The variegated form is the most ornamental and comes in miniature and standard sizes that range from 1 to 2½ feet tall. Flowers are insignificant. Use as a vertical accent plant in pools of any size. Grow in full sun or partial shade in wet soil or in water up to 6 inches deep. Hardy in Zones 4 to 10.

Thalia *(Thalia dealbata)*　This native American bog plant offers bold, upright foliage and graceful spikes of tiny, purple flowers in summer. Reaches 7 or more feet tall, but stays about 3 to 4 feet tall if contained. This is an excellent plant grouped in the background of a water garden. Or use as a broad-leaved accent plant, especially appealing in front of stonework. Grow in full sun or partial shade in wet soil or in water up to 12 inches deep.

Water arum (*Peltandra virginica*)

The brittle stems are easily broken. Hardy in Zones 6 to 10.

Water arum *(Peltandra virginica)*　The glossy dark green leaves of the water arum are arrow-shaped and rise from short fleshy roots. The summer-blooming flowers are pea-green spathes with a white spadix and resemble jack-in-the-pulpit blossoms. Grows about 2 feet tall. Use these vigorous plants in masses to decorate the edges of a large pool or stream. Grow in full sun or partial shade in wet soil or in up to 6 inches of water. Hardy in Zones 5 to 10.

Water clover *(Marsilea species)*　Resembling clusters of four-leaf clovers floating on the water, these interesting plants are actually ferns. Also called four-leaf clover plant, it adds a beautiful texture to the water surface. The 2- to 3-inch-wide leaves are green with brown and yellow variegations. Plants

Water clover (*Marsilea* species)

White bulrush (*Scirpus albescens*)

Water hawthorn (*Aponogeton distachyus*)

Water pennywort (*Hydrocotyle vulgaris*)

trail across the water surface, rooting where they can. Weed out excess growth to keep within bounds. Transplants well and does well in shade where other aquatics may have a difficult time. Hardy in Zones 6 to 10. Grow in 4- to 12-inch-deep water.

Water hawthorn *(Aponogeton distachyus)* Also called cape pondweed, this reliable aquatic has green strap-shaped leaves spotted with purple. These float on the water surface. The oddly forked blossoms are white with black stamens and give off a strong vanilla scent. Flowers bloom in spring and fall, as well as in winter in Zones 9 and 10. Plant in containers set 4 to 12 inches below the water surface in partial to moderate shade. Hardy in Zones 5 to 10.

Water pennywort *(Hydrocotyle vulgaris)* This charming plant creeps across wet soil or stands just above the water sur-

face. Foliage is umbrella-shaped, resembling nasturtium leaves, and ½ to 2 inches across. Clusters of wispy greenish white flowers appear in early to midsummer. Use to create a contrasting texture on the water surface in pools of any size. Grow in damp soil or in water up to 8 inches deep. May be invasive; weed out if necessary. Hardy in Zones 8 to 10.

White bulrush *(Scirpus albescens)* Superb as a vertical accent in a mass planting, white bulrush lends a natural marshy look to a water garden. The 2- to 6-foot tall cylindrical leaves are striped cream and green, giving it a pale green, almost white, appearance from a distance. Drooping tassels of brown flowers appear in mid- to late summer. Use in the background or corners of a medium-sized or large pool. Grow in full sun in humid climates, in partial shade in dry climates. Needs wet soil or water up to 6 inches deep. Hardy in Zones 5 to 10.

Bog lily (*Crinum americanum*)

Giant Egyptian papyrus (*Cyperus papyrus*)

Creeping water primrose (*Ludwigia palustris*)

Spider lily (*Hymenocallis* species)

VARIETIES OF TROPICAL BOG AND MARGINAL PLANTS

The tropical bog plants described here include a wide range of flowering and foliage plants, ranging in size from the tall, distinctive umbrella palm to the diminutive water poppy, with its bright yellow flowers. The heights given are those that are expected for container-grown plants; plants grown in large containers or in earth-bottomed ponds will be larger. All of the plants listed here are tender and will be killed by frost or cold weather; they can, however, be grown as annuals as far north as Zone 3. The entry for each plant indicates in which zones it is perennial, living through the winter.

Bog lily *(Crinum americanum)* Native to the swamps of Texas and Florida, bog lily has long straplike leaves and enchanting white flowers in summer. The unusual flowers consist of drooping petals and sepals united in a tubular base. Clumps reach 2 feet tall. Use as a specimen plant when in bloom. Grow in full sun or partial shade, in wet soil or in water up to 6 inches deep. Hardy in Zones 8 to 10.

Creeping water primrose *(Ludwigia palustris)* Creeping water primrose roots in shallow water and on muddy banks. Its long stems are covered with brilliant green foliage. Bright yellow flowers measure ¾ inch across and bloom in spring. Can be invasive. Control by pinching and pruning. Hardy in Zones 9 and 10.

Papyrus *(Cyperus* species) Dwarf papyrus (*Cyperus isocladus*) produces tufts of linear foliage at the tips of 1½ to 2-foot-tall stems. Giant Egyptian papyrus (*Cyperus papyrus*) grows to a dramatic height of 6 to 10 feet. The feathery leaves top these tall stems and make an impressive background in a large pool. Both have wheat-colored flowers that

Violet-stemmed taro (*Colocasia esculenta* var. *fontanesii*)

Water canna (*Canna* hybrid)

Umbrella palm (*Cyperus alternifolius*)

bloom among the leaves in summer. Clumps remain neat and provide an interesting foliage contrast to bolder-textured plants. Use dwarf payrus as an accent in small to medium-sized pools. Plant giant Egyptian papyrus in large tubs and use in the corners or in the center of a large pool. Both grow in full sun or partial shade in wet soil or in water up to 6 inches deep. Hardy in Zones 9 and 10, but may be overwintered indoors as houseplants or in a greenhouse in colder climates, if the containers are kept standing in water.

Spider lily *(Hymenocallis species)*   The spider-shaped, white flowers of the spider lily bloom in spring and summer and have a delightful fragrance. Foliage is upright to 2 feet tall. Grow as a specimen plant while in bloom and then move to the background. Place in full sun or partial shade in water up to 6 inches deep. Hardy in Zones 8 to 10.

Taro *(Colocasia esculenta)*   Used in ornamental gardens primarily for its huge arrowhead-shaped, dark green foliage, green taro offers the additional attraction of edible tubers. One of the staple foods of the Hawaiian islands, poi is made from cooked, pounded tubers. Tubers must be properly cooked or they are toxic. Violet-stemmed taro (*C. esculenta* var. *fontanesii*) is similar but with eye-catching dark violet stems. The plant may reach 3½ feet tall, or 6 feet in a greenhouse. Flowers are inconspicuous golden spathes. Use as a bold accent plant in full sun or partial shade. Grow in wet soil or in water up to 12 inches deep. Hardy in Zones 9 and 10.

Umbrella palm *(Cyperus alternifolius)*   Grown for its distinctive whorls of foliage atop 3- to 4-foot-tall stems, umbrella palm is a favorite aquatic plant. It resembles dwarf papyrus, but the foliage is broader and stems are taller. Use as a background in medium-sized or large pools or as an accent in a small pool. May be invasive. Grow in full sun, partial shade, or filtered light. Plant in wet soil or in water up to 6 inches deep. Hardy in Zones 9 and 10, but can be treated as a tender aquatic and overwintered as a houseplant if kept wet and given enough light.

Water canna *(Canna hybrids)*   The eye-catching, summer flowers of the water canna come in shades of pink, red, orange, and yellow. Foliage is swordlike and reaches 4 feet tall. Plant is massed for best effect. Needs full sun and wet soil or water up to 6 inches deep. Hardy in Zones 7 to 10.

Anacharis (*Elodea canadensis*)

Cabomba (*Cabomba caroliniana*)

SUBMERGED PLANTS

The roots of submerged plants are anchored in soil, but their delicate green leaves stay underwater rather than floating on the surface. Submerged plants are distinguished by their foliage, which may be fernlike, lacy, hairlike, or long-leaved. Since they release oxygen directly into the water, they are frequently referred to as *oxygenating plants*. All are flowering plants, but their blossoms are insignificant and often are unnoticed.

Though not grown for show, submerged plants belong in almost every garden pool. They play a vital role in balancing the ecology of a pond by competing with algae for dissolved nutrients and carbon dioxide. In new pools, where the water is rich in minerals, submerged plants grow rapidly. They use up nutrients and carbon dioxide and shade the water, discouraging the growth of algae that cloud the water. Submerged plants offer another benefit—their grassy leaves provide food and a natural spawning area for fish.

Growing Submerged Plants

For submerged plants, the planting procedures are similar to those for planting water lilies. However, submerged plants require less soil and the soil should contain a high proportion of sand or gravel. Do not fertilize the soil since these submerged plants get all the nutrients they need from dissolved minerals in the pool water.

These plants are sold in bunches of six stems, by the dozen, or in hundreds. Plant a 5-quart pail with five or six bunches of plants. Place the containers in the pool so that the leaves are submerged to a depth of between 6 and 16 inches. If planted directly in an earth-bottomed pond, they will spread rapidly.

Submerged plants help keep the water clear of algae. To be effective, the plants should occupy about one-third of the total volume of the pool. Since they grow and spread very rapidly, you can begin with a maximum of one plant for every 1 or 2 square feet of pond surface. Plant several bunches of plants together. For an 8 foot by 5 foot pond, you'll need six 10-quart containers with ten bunches of plants in each.

Varieties of Submerged Plants

The varieties described below are suitable for North American gardens and are readily available from water-garden suppliers.

Anacharis (*Elodea canadensis*) This deep green plant has whorls of delicate leaves that remain beneath the water surface and make an ideal spot for spawning fish. Fish also love to eat the foliage, especially during winter. Will grow in water 6 inches to 5 feet deep, in full sun, partial shade, or filtered light. Hardy in Zones 5 to 10.

Cabomba (*Cabomba caroliniana*) The bright green underwater foliage of cabomba, also called fanwort, grows in graceful fans. Tiny white flowers bloom in summer. Fish spawn among the leaves in spring and early summer and baby fish find the foliage an attractive, cool hiding place. Grows best in filtered light but tolerates both partial shade and full sun. Does best in cool water up to 30

Dwarf sagittaria (*Sagittaria natans*)

Vallisneria (*Vallisneria americana*)

inches deep; does poorly in shallow water or in raised pools, which can become hot. Hardy in Zones 6 to 10.

Dwarf sagittaria *(Sagittaria natans)*
This plant has translucent, green straplike leaves that look decorative in clear water. A good oxygenator but doesn't provide enough cover for fish spawning. Leaves grow 3 to 6 inches long. Plant in water 6 to 30 inches deep in full sun, partial shade, or filtered light. Hardy in Zones 5 to 10.

Vallisneria *(Vallisneria americana)*
Also called tape grass and ribbon grass, vallisneria has ribbonlike, translucent pale green leaves. These are decorative as well as practical, providing food and shelter for fish and filtering the water. Flowers are tiny and insignificant. Grow in shade, partial shade, or sun in water 6 to 24 inches deep. Winter-dormant in all climates. Hardy in Zones 4 to 10.

Water milfoil *(Myriophyllum* species)*
These excellent oxygenators may have green or reddish hairlike foliage that is useful for trapping debris and for fish spawning. Grows in full sun, partial shade, or filtered light in still or running water from 6 to 30 inches deep. Hardy in Zones 5 to 10.

FLOATING PLANTS

Also useful for adorning a garden pool are floating plants. These don't need any soil—their roots hang into the water while their small leaves and blossoms bob on the surface. Admired for their foliage and flowers, floating

Water milfoil (*Myriophyllum* species)

plants contrast well with the bold foliage and flowers of water lilies.

Growing Floating Plants

Floating plants are sold by the bunch. They are easy to grow—simply float them on the surface of the pond and they take care of

Shellflower (*Pistia stratiotes*)

Water poppy (*Hydrocleys nymphoides*)

themselves. If they reproduce too quickly and overrun the surface or crowd other plants, weed them out. They can be pulled out by hand or pulled out with a net.

Varieties of Floating Plants

The floating plants described here are easy to grow and will add to the variety of plants in your pool.

Shellflower *(Pistia stratiotes)* Also called water lettuce, this unusual plant resembles a velvety Boston lettuce floating on the water. The pale green foliage grows in rosettes and baby plants sprout from the sides. A whole colony may develop by summer's end. Mature plants reach about 6 inches across. This floating plant makes a beautiful textural contrast to other aquatics. Develops best color in shade, but likes heat and humidity. Interstate shipments are forbidden in some states because of its potential to become a nuisance in natural waterways. Propagate by dividing offsets. Hardy in Zones 9 and 10.

Water hyacinth *(Eichhornia crassipes)* Water hyacinth's pale lavender clusters of butterflylike flowers bloom on raised spikes in midsummer. The shiny green foliage has swollen leaf bases that give this floating plant its buoyancy. Trailing roots make an ideal spawning site for fish. Water hyacinth is so prolific that it is an efficient water purifier. It uses up excess water nutrients and balances the pH, slowing algae growth. Unfortunately, this pretty plant can be invasive and is a serious nuisance in waterways in warm climates.

Water hyacinth (*Eichhornia crassipes*)

Its transportation across state lines is forbidden. Do not grow this plant in warm climates if there is any possibility of its escaping to a natural pond or stream. You can safely grow water hyacinth in northern climates where it will be killed by frost if it escapes to the wild. Grow in full sun. Hardy in Zones 9 and 10.

Water poppy *(Hydrocleys nymphoides)* The deep yellow, 3-petalled flowers of the water poppy measure 2 inches across. They are held out of the water just above the floating foliage. Leaves are round, 1 to 3 inches across. Plants spread by stolons, trailing across the water surface like a strawberry plant and will sometimes root in shallow water. Use in masses on the water surface in front of upright plants. Weed out excess growth. Grow in full sun or partial shade. Because they can become pests in natural waterways in warm climates, water poppies may not be transported into California. Hardy in Zones 8 to 10.

SELECTING AQUATIC PLANTS

In planning your water garden, consider the mix of plants. You can give free expression to your own preferences for texture, fragrance, and color. The aquatic plants detailed in this chapter are available from many nurseries or mail-order supply houses. Unlike the plants suggested in most books on water gardening, many of which were written by British authors, the aquatic plants included in this book are available in North America and are adapted to climates here.

Some water-garden suppliers offer a "starter collection" of plants for ponds of various sizes. This may be a good way to begin. Later, you can add to the collection or replace plants. If you are putting together your own starter collection, be sure to maintain a balance between submerged and surface plants. To achieve a balanced pool, keep the following information in mind when making your selection of aquatic plants.

No more than 70 percent of the water surface should be covered with leaves of aquatic plants, less in larger pools. Since a large water lily may spread over more than 8 square feet, one or two plants may be the maximum for your pond. For a small pond look for the pygmy hybrids that spread over about 3 feet

Above: The surface of this small pool is an eye-catching pattern of foliage colors, shapes, and sizes highlighted by soft-colored blossoms. Included are 'Comanche' and 'Marliacea Albida' hardy water lilies, water hawthorn, and iris.

Left: This selection of aquatic plants is so appealing because it successfully combines foliage with fine and bold textures and round and elongated shapes. Included are 'Sultan' water lily, lotus, parrot's-feather, giant papyrus, sweet flag, and water hyacinth.

Fish are fun to watch and care for and also help control mosquitoes and algae. Here, koi share the pool with the hardy water lilies 'Marliacea Carnea' and 'Sultan'.

or miniatures that spread only a foot. Sizes specified in the plant descriptions may vary somewhat depending on the size of the container, the type of plant food you use, the amount of sunlight the plant receives, and the length of your growing season.

For an average-sized garden pool measuring 6 feet by 8 feet and 2 feet deep, a proper mix of aquatics might be:

☐ 3 water lilies

☐ 3 surface plants, such as floating-heart

☐ 3 surface plants, such as parrot's-feather, with contrasting texture

☐ 16 marginal plants with a vertical habit, such as iris or dwarf papyrus

☐ 36 bunches of submerged plants

FISH IN A GARDEN POND

For anyone who enjoys gazing into a still, sunlit pool, darting fish are the glittering prizes. Whether hovering suspended over a frilly whorl of submerged grass, restlessly seeking out tidbits of food, or racing about in the frenzy of the mating chase, fish are star performers in the underwater world. Some gardeners install pools purely for the pleasure of stocking them with unusual varieties of ornamental fish. Whether or not you develop a connoisseur's instinct for the rare and unusual, you will quickly come to look for their

graceful, darting bodies. The glint of their scales is a constant reminder of the brisk pace of life that goes on beneath the water surface.

Many kinds of small, hardy fish thrive in a modest-sized pond. They can be trained to respond to signals for feeding, and they will "come to dinner" at the sight of their care giver or when someone taps on the side of the pool. Varieties of cold-water fish range in size from small, young goldfish to giant koi. Koi can attain 2 feet in length when mature; some will reach 3 feet in large pools.

Preparing the Pond for Fish

Before placing any fish in a new pool, you need to ensure their survival. Allow fresh tap or well water to stand for 24 hours so that it can reach the ambient temperature. Treat the tap water with DeChlor® or a similar agent to remove all traces of chlorine compounds (see page 28).

As an added precaution, if you have used concrete or mortar anywhere around the pond, take a pH reading to determine whether the water has turned alkaline from an excess of lime. Inexpensive pH testing kits are widely available and the test is a simple process.

In general, a pH reading above 8.5 indicates that the water probably contains dissolved concrete, which will be harmful or deadly to fish. Any reading between 6.5 and 8.5 is usually safe, though each fish species has its own range of tolerance. Where well water is naturally alkaline, with a pH range from 7.5 to 8.5, fish and plants usually have no problems because the water's chemistry is such that nutrients are available. But if the alkalinity is increased by dissolved concrete, the water chemistry changes and fish suffer. After a new pool has been leached properly, there should be no more problems (see page 29).

The young fish will need floating and submerged leaves to shelter them from direct sunlight, especially if the pool is less than 36 inches deep, and is not shaded by trees or a building. However, before stocking your pond you'll also need to consider the welfare of the plants. Fish feed on the tender leaves of submerged plants. Allow several weeks for the young plants to establish themselves before introducing fish. If you want to stock fish and plants at the same time, buy established plants in containers.

Overcrowding can threaten the lives and welfare of young fish, especially when they are getting adjusted to the new environment. As a rule, the maximum stocking rate is 1 inch of fish for every 3 to 5 gallons of water. For example, a pond holding five hundred gallons would accommodate thirty-three 3-inch-long fish. After three or four months, if those fish are doing well, you might introduce a few more. But remember that the stock you have will grow and probably spawn every year.

Since ornamental fish are usually shipped in large quantities in sealed containers, they are under stress and, therefore, more susceptible to disease. There is some risk of introducing fungus, parasites, or disease whenever you add new fish to your pool. Always disinfect the pool with Argucide® or Desa Fin® before introducing new stock. Better yet, quarantine and medicate the new fish in a separate holding container for two weeks and watch for signs of illness.

When fish arrive or when you buy them, check them carefully to make sure there are no fluffy white areas on their backs, which is a sign of fungus. Also examine their tails for fin rot, evidenced by ragged edges. Beware of closed fins and reddened areas around gills or elsewhere. Fish rubbing themselves and flipping against the pool bottom when swimming are exhibiting a behavior called *flashing,* which indicates parasites. Any fish with these symptoms and any that appear lethargic should be rejected.

Introducing Fish to Your Pond

Fish cannot be introduced immediately to the pool; they must first be acclimatized to the water temperature. Although hardy fish can adjust to a range of temperature, a sudden shock to their systems as they enter a pool that is even a few degrees colder than their body temperature can cause death. Fish are usually shipped in a sealed bag that also contains their oxygen supply. Before opening the bag, set it on the surface of the pond for 15 minutes to allow it to adjust to the pool temperature. On a sunny day, cover the bag with a towel to prevent it from overheating.

Upon being released, fish that normally swim near the surface may dive straight for the bottom looking for shelter. Unless they are naturally scavenger fish, they will soon rise toward the surface and begin swimming about looking for food.

Caring for Hardy Pool Fish

Unlike many tropical breeds of aquarium fish, which cannot endure cold water, hardy ornamental fish can be left in the pool all year around. The metabolism of fish changes with the temperature of the water. In summer they are most active and feed frequently, so you can supplement their natural supply of food (submerged leaves, algae, and insect larvae) with fish food. Four or five times a week, or every day if you like, sprinkle fish food in the water. As a rule, do not give them more than they will eat in about five minutes, because the extra food will sink to the bottom and begin to decay. Even in summer, fish can be left without food for several weeks at a time. They will survive quite well on submerged plants, insects, and algae.

As fall approaches and the water cools, fish will feed more heavily and more frequently as they stock up for winter. When the water cools below 45° F, however, the fish stop feeding entirely and become less active. Throughout the winter, they are almost dormant and are not interested in food. In spring, when the water temperature rises above 45° F, they resume normal feeding.

Most owners enjoy feeding their fish, although it is unnecessary since ornamental fish can survive quite well on only algae and insects.

As long as ice does not completely cover the pond for weeks at a time, fish can remain outdoors through the winter. If the ice forms a solid layer, carbon dioxide builds up underneath it, and the fish will eventually die from lack of oxygen. This problem occurs most frequently in pools containing decaying leaves and other organic matter, which release large quantities of carbon dioxide into the water. In a clean pool, fish can survive beneath a solid layer of ice for a week or so.

To help fish survive, clear your pool of decaying plant matter as winter approaches. Also make sure that there is always an area of unfrozen water on the surface. Thaw a hole in the ice occasionally or install an automatic deicer that is activated by a thermostatically controlled switch when the water temperature drops to within a few degrees of freezing. A heating coil keeps a small area clear of ice. Be sure never to break the ice; the blow could kill the fish. (See pages 105 to 106 for more information on controlling ice.)

Spawning

In temperate zones, fish spawn in the late spring or early summer. The first physiological changes appear in the male and female when the water temperature approaches 60° F. Raised white tubercles about the size of

pinheads appear on the gill plates of the males. Females fatten visibly as their ovaries fill with eggs. Spawning, which usually begins at sunup and ends by noon, consists of several vigorous underwater chases. After each chase, the female releases thousands of eggs coated with a sticky substance; the eggs adhere to the nearest object, usually a submerged plant. The male immediately releases sperm, called milt, over the eggs and they are fertilized. Within four or five days, the fry hatch. These young fish attach themselves to the plants or the sides of the pool and feed off their yolk sacs for several days.

Since many of the fry die or are devoured by insects or mature fish, only two or three from each spawning can be expected to live to the next season. To ensure a greater survival rate, purchase a spawning mat from a watergarden or fish supplier. Made from an artificial material resembling Spanish moss, the rectangular spawning mat attracts fertile fish, especially if submerged plant material is scarce. The gray fish eggs adhering to the black mat are easy to spot. After the fish have finished spawning, transfer the mat to a separate pool where there are no large fish and the fry will be protected. Feed the small fish with crumbled flake food or brine shrimp until they are 1 inch long.

VARIETIES OF FISH

Fish for your garden pool come in numerous colors, varieties, and sizes. You can obtain them from specialty mail-order suppliers or at pet or aquarium stores. Fish from a shop may have difficulty adjusting to outdoor temperatures since they are used to living in a controlled environment.

Goldfish

Goldfish are the most popular and inexpensive of outdoor pond fish. Their ultimate size depends upon their surroundings. Those confined to a fish bowl stay small; those in an outdoor pool can grow to 10 to 12 inches in length, or more. Goldfish usually have shiny red or orange scales, but are sometimes yellow or white. Some varieties have distinctive black, blue, or silver markings as well, but dramatic dark markings can be almost invisible in an outdoor pool, since the mottled coloration blends with the pool color.

Shubunkins are a variety of goldfish colored a striking blue or blue-gray. Their bodies may also be mottled red, blue, black-brown, and white. Comets may be colored like regular goldfish but they sport flowing tails often as long as their bodies. Fantails have short, egg-shaped bodies adorned with a beautiful double tail fin that creates an attractive wavy pattern as they swim.

One kind of fantail, the Chinese Moor, is entirely black and has large, telescopic eyes. Though a dramatic contrast to the brightly colored fish around it, the black Moor may be hard to see in a deep pool. All these varieties are goldfish, so they will interbreed. Unless the stock is carefully maintained, and all the mongrel fish of mixed colors removed, the offspring will eventually begin to look alike.

Golden Orfe

The slender salmon-colored fish called the golden orfe (*Leuciscus idus*) is a variety of the silver-colored common orfe. Because of its shimmering salmon-gold color, it is highly visible. It is also very active and prefers to swim in shoals, or groups. The golden orfe will dart at any insect that touches the water surface, and it may jump right out of the pond and play in the spray of a fountain or waterfall. Maturing to a length of a foot or more, golden orfes do best in ponds at least 5 feet long where

there is plenty of room for their playful activities. Orfe cannot be imported to some states with mild climates, lest they escape to a natural waterway where they could reproduce so quickly that they would compete with desirable game fish. It is a good idea to check your local ordinances before stocking your pool with these fish.

Koi

The largest of the hardy pond fish, koi commonly grow to 2 feet long, but can reach 3 feet under certain conditions. These dramatic Japanese carp have shiny scales and come in a

Above: Shubunkin goldfish sport long, flowing tails and a mottled pattern of various colors. Below: Fantail goldfish are admired for their wide, translucent tails and fins that wave gracefully as they swim and dive.

Above: Pet cats may try to "fish" in your garden pool or may simply sunbathe on the warm rocks. Below: Children delight in caring for pet goldfish. Supervise youngsters closely; raised pools are the safest. Opposite: Koi can reach several feet in length, but in most garden pools, they mature at 1½ to 2 feet.

range of iridescent colors including red, orange, yellow, pink, and white. Bronze, steel-blue, and gray varieties look as if they are covered with metallic armor. Collectors pay high prices for rare varieties of koi, but most varieties are not expensive.

Because they will eventually grow large, koi are best suited to pools at least 4 by 6 feet in size and 16 inches deep, though they can be kept in smaller pools. When confined to a small pool, they will not grow as large as they might with more space. Koi swim in groups and are easily trained. Koi are long-lived, commonly surviving for twenty or thirty years;

some have been documented to live for more than two hundred years.

Other Fish

Though goldfish, golden orfe, and koi are the showiest fish you can keep in your pond, other varieties offer diversity. Mosquito fish (*Gambusia affinis*) are not cold hardy, but are suitable for mild climates and eat a lot of insects. Big mouth bass, catfish, and bluegill may also be kept in a garden pool but will eat other fish.

OTHER AQUATIC ANIMALS

Snails, tadpoles, freshwater clams, and mussels are also recommended for naturalistic garden pools; they act as scavengers that help to clean the bottom of a pool. Freshwater mussels—sometimes called "nature's own filter system"—will help remedy green or cloudy pool water.

Though snails don't do much for water clarity one way or the other, they are interesting to have around. The best variety is the black Japanese snail (*Viviparus malleatus*). Bearing live young, it breeds in modest numbers, so it will never overrun the pool. These snails do not leave the pond; they will not crawl out and invade your lawn and garden nor will they eat aquatic plants.

Tadpoles provide entertainment for children, who can watch them grow into frogs. Tadpoles help clean the pool and later, when they become frogs, they help control the insect population. The tadpoles that may appear in your pond uninvited, however, will not necessarily be bullfrog tadpoles; they may grow into common garden toads instead. Bullfrog tadpoles may be ordered from a water-garden supply house.

Once your pool is planted and stocked, it takes little care to keep the plants and fish flourishing. An added enjoyment will be that more songbirds will come to your yard, splashing in the pool's edge as they drink and bathe. And, if you live near large bodies of natural water, ducks and other water birds may come for a visit, too. Don't encourage these to stay, however, because waterfowl can pollute the water and devastate your fish population. Raccoons, and occasionally pet cats, may fish in your garden pool, too. If these animals are a problem, better avoid those high-priced koi!

Landscaping Your Garden Pool

Create a lovely setting to enhance your garden's focal point.

Every garden pool deserves a setting that enhances its appearance. Your aim is to make the water garden belong in its setting and not seem to be an isolated element in your garden. You can do this by connecting the water feature to the rest of the garden with a path, a patio, or planting beds. A distant backdrop of trees and shrubs and a border of low-growing plants tie the pool in with the rest of your landscape.

In landscaping your water garden, you will want to create harmonious relationships among the water feature, the architectural character of your home, and the rest of your yard and garden. Landscape designers emphasize that all the elements of a garden should work together. That means that the color scheme, style, and structures should complement each other. You might want to echo the color of your house trim with similar-colored garden structures and include some flowers that are in the same color group.

If your pool is formal and symmetrical, the paving, garden beds, plants, lawn, and patio areas should emphasize its neat, clean lines and balanced shape. A formal pool often requires more man-made structures than plants around it. Keep it uncluttered. Use aquatic or marginal plants to accent the lines of the pool and fountain, not to compete with them. In a formal garden, the colors and placement of edging materials create distinctive patterns that complement the geometry of the pool. Neatly planted beds of flowers could add bright accents of color. A well-tended lawn lends a sense of spaciousness and distance to your garden; closely planted, pruned shrubs create a more intimate feeling.

The earth-colored stone patio, the redwood dining set, and the skillful placement of tropical plants enhance the quiet beauty of this pond's desert setting.

A natural pool calls for rocky borders, loose-textured plants, and casual transitions from one area to the next. Many different naturalistic landscape effects can be created around an informal water garden. Though the area around a man-made garden pool is no wetter than the rest of your lawn or garden, you can simulate a wetland with ornamental grasses and interesting bog plants. You might even recreate a desert oasis and cactus garden. A waterfall surrounded by a rock garden of alpine plants can look like a mountain stream. Overhung with blossoms and the lush foliage of wildflowers and ferns, the same waterway might resemble a brook in a shady forest or tropical grove. The effects are limitless, depending only on your creativity and the space available.

Every garden is different, so there are no firm rules to be followed except that of planning in advance. Using graph paper, you can create a scale drawing of your property and plot out the placement of each element. Some garden themes and border treatments are suggested by the illustrations and photographs in this chapter.

EDGING MATERIALS

The edge of a pool is defined and camouflaged by the materials that you place around it. For a formal pond you might want to install an edging—called coping—of brick, flagstone, wood, Belgian blocks, or paving stone. (For more information on the types of paving materials that are available in your area, visit a local quarry or a stone yard.) The best colors for bordering materials are grays, browns, dark terra-cottas, and other earth tones. Avoid white stones, which would compete with the brightness of the water and look unnatural. The border of a formal pool acts as a frame; too light a paving draws the eye away from the central focal point.

If you decide on brickwork, you might want to use worn bricks that have darkened with age to match already existing brickwork in your yard. A wooden deck at the side of a pool should be made of lumber that has been pressure-treated, not dipped in a toxic preservative. Cedar is a beautiful but more expensive choice. Redwood must be weathered gray or it may poison the pond. Should you decide to

Opposite above: Dramatic in its simplicity this reflective pool matches the bold architectural lines and the formal feeling of the house. Opposite below: The clean corners of the flagstone edging sustain the formal feeling of this garden pool. By overhanging the water, the flagstone camouflages the liner of the pool.

Mimicking a series of pools in an alpine meadow, this garden offers a naturalistic setting for growing rock garden plants.

A small garden pool becomes the centerpiece of a colorful flower garden composed of annuals and perennials.

The cool depths of this garden pool and the colorful plants along its edges transform this desert cactus garden into a welcoming oasis.

Above: A natural setting is enhanced by candytuft and blue fescue in the crevices of the fieldstone edging. Aquatic plants include creeping water primrose, tropical water lilies, cattail, and pickerel rush. Below: A deck overhanging a large pond provides a perfect sitting area. Aquatics include pickerel rush, iris, and night-blooming tropical water lilies.

have two kinds of paving materials around the border, such as brick and wood, or brick and dark flagstone, take the time to look at actual samples of the materials together before you place them over a wide area, to make sure that their colors and textures are compatible.

Consider also how the materials will look if used near your house. Colors, textures, and style should complement the colors of your siding and trim, and the design should be suitable for the architecture of your home. In general, be very selective in choosing coping, paving, patio, and terrace materials since they will become a permanent part of the landscape and a mistake would be costly.

Installing Coping Around a Formal Pool

Coping is the edge of the pavement that outlines the contours of the pool. The paving material used for the coping should cover up the edge of the liner and hang over the edge of the pool by 2 inches, though this cannot always be done if irregular rocks are used. The overhang makes the liner less visible and helps protect it from sunlight. It is important to prepare a mortar footing for the coping material, especially in areas where the ground freezes hard in winter or is subject to heavy foot traffic.

To create a firm foundation for stone to be set around a lined pool, excavate the soil bordering the pool so that you can pour in a 2- to 4-inch layer of reinforced concrete and top that with the coping. Trim the excess PVC so that 12 inches of liner overlap into the coping excavation. (Save some of the extra PVC for patches.) Spread a 2-inch layer of mortar reinforced with rebar into the excavation, covering the overlapping liner. Set the bricks, stones, or whatever you are using in the mortar so that the edges of the paving material are cantilevered out over the water, if possible. Spread mortar between the stones.

Around a fiberglass pool, install coping in a similar manner. The coping should overhang the edge of the pool by 2 inches to hide the fiberglass sides. For circular or curved PVC or fiberglass pools, use a masonry chisel to shape the coping stones so that they follow the contour of the pool. You may need some practice in chiseling stone without shattering it, so purchase extra material if you plan to do it yourself. Bricks and other small paving materials will not need to be shaped if you place them close together. Set the bricks so they can fan outward on the curves, then fill in spaces with mortar.

Edging an Informal Pool

Unlike the symmetrical, paved border that looks best around a formal pool, the informal border is usually made up of multitextured plants and rocks, or even grass. There are numerous ways to obscure the transition from water to land so that the edge of the liner is concealed and anchored and the pool still looks natural. The best edging materials include irregularly shaped paving slabs, bark chips, pebbles, rocks, and boulders. You can form an irregular coping with large slabs of flat stone, or create a sloped, pebbled beach with a few boulders placed near the water's edge. On one side, turf grass can come all the way to the edge of the water; the opposite bank can be planted with wildflowers. Or you can create an alpine rock garden that climbs the grade beside a pool or waterfall.

The secret to achieving a natural-looking pool is in the placement of the rocks. Bury them slightly so that they emerge from the ground; don't simply set them on top. For the best effect, group rocks randomly, not in a single row around the edge of the water.

An informal water-garden landscape is also more flexible than is the permanent arrangement of paved and planted areas around a formal pool. Around an informal pond, plantings can be rearranged seasonally, rocks can be shifted, and graveled or pebbled areas can easily be expanded or reduced in size.

EDGING AND BACKGROUND PLANTS

Before introducing any plants, consider their ideal location in terms of sunlight, soil, and moisture as well as garden design. Choose plants suited to your climate and your garden's conditions. Though bog and moisture-loving plants look at home near a water garden, the site may not offer them ideal growing conditions.

Border plants should be situated so that they do not obscure the water and the water lilies. This means that tall plants are best

Rocks and boulders sunk slightly below the water level of an informal pool create a naturalistic look as well as camouflage the pool liner.

A PVC liner underlies this pebbled beach, which is sloped to channel rainwater into the stream that flows into a large pond. The liner also prevents weeds from growing among the pebbles.

Edging With Lawn

E dging a garden pond with grass is tricky because surrounding soil may wash into the water. Using sod rather than seed helps solve this problem.

Dig a shallow trench around the pool's perimeter and let the PVC from the pool extend into the trench. The PVC edge should slope down and away from the pool in order to keep out water runoff. Overlap the PVC with sod by about 2 inches.

If you're digging the pool in an existing lawn, carefully carve the shape of the pool and strip back the sod as you excavate. When you're ready to finish the edges, the sod should fit perfectly around the pool.

placed on the far side of a pool or in small foreground clumps. Avoid ringing the pool with thick foliage and tall stems. You can mingle areas of open lawn with beds of flowers and ferns, or plant low-spreading shrubs or ground covers near the water.

Drifts of several varieties of spreading plants and just a few accent plants create the most pleasing effect. Too many different kinds of plants can make the garden appear confusing and busy. Frame your garden pool with masses of similar plants and you'll make it the center of attraction.

Larger plants, such as trees and shrubs, should be selected judiciously, since by their size they will dominate the landscape. Plant them as a background to the water garden, but not overhanging its edge or you may hide the water from view. Leaves falling in the pool can also be a problem if you plant too closely. If you want to grow water lilies, trees ought to be placed to the north of a pool, so they will not shade the water. Trees to the south of a pool should be far enough away so that they will not block the sunlight once they are full grown. For planting close to the edge of a pond, evergreens are recommended as long as they don't shade the water, since they drop fewer leaves than do deciduous trees.

A tree to be avoided is the weeping willow. Though it is picturesque alongside a natural stream, it eventually grows too big to be well suited to all but the largest artificial ponds. And water-seeking roots of the willow can damage the pool's liner. Willow leaves drop continuously and contain chemicals that can kill fish. To create an effect similar to that of a weeping willow, plant a weeping cherry tree, which won't grow as large. Other toxic trees to be avoided are California and Brazilian pepper trees (*Schinus* sp.).

PLANTING SITES

The border of a water garden may have several distinct areas, with varying amounts of sun, shade, and moisture. So that your garden will thrive, study your site before choosing plants. Although shade- and moisture-loving plants look most natural around the edge of a pool, the soil around an artificial pool is no moister than it would be without the pool. It will have to be specially prepared as a bog garden if you want water-loving plants to thrive there (see page 83). Many varieties of waterside plants need to have wet soil and full sunlight. These are perfect for a bog planting in an open space at one end of a water-lily pond. Other moisture-loving plants may require shade or partial shade and can be grown under the overhanging limbs of high-pruned trees. You may have to pay extra attention to keeping them well watered, but no other special conditions are needed. Included in this group are many varieties of irises and tall ornamental grasses, as well as lower plants such as hostas and ferns.

A sunny water-lily pond is the perfect site for a border of sun-loving flowers. You can plant many kinds of perennials in permanent

beds or containers. Flowering annuals also flourish in full sun. A rock garden can accommodate many hardy alpine plants, which flourish on high mountain slopes, or succulents such as sempervivums. Smaller, shade-loving varieties of wildflowers may be grown in a shadier garden, especially along a stream or waterfall.

If your pool or water garden is in a woodland setting, you have a perfect place for ferns, hostas, azaleas, and rhododendrons, as well as many kinds of forest wildflowers. Generally, these plants require loamy, acidic soil enriched with peat or humus. Many shade-loving plants will tolerate wet roots and can be grown in a boggy area. Azaleas and rhododendrons, however, should be planted in moist but well-drained soil.

Choosing Plants
For Your Landscape

On the pages that follow you will find charts of landscape plants that are effectively used around water gardens. The lists include perennials, shrubs, trees, and ground covers. When selecting plants from these charts, check the hardiness zone to make sure the plants are suited to your part of the country.

Trees shouldn't overhang a garden pool or shade the water. Tall trees, like this palm tree, are best located at a distance and to the north of a pond in order to leave the water in full sun.

Succulents and tropical plants flourish around this concrete water-lily pool in a warm California garden.

An Environment For Bog Plants

Numerous woodland, marsh, and swamp plants flourish in boggy soil where their roots remain constantly moist. You can establish a bog at the edge of a garden pool, but if the two share the same water source, silt may move from the boggy area into the pond, so it is best to separate the pool from the bog with a natural sill of garden soil or with a paved walk. Create an artificial bog by underlying the garden site with PVC or 500-gauge plastic sheeting to keep the soil wet. Excavate the bog garden to a depth of 9 inches and spread the sheeting across the bottom and 6 inches up the sides.

Though you should take reasonable precautions to prevent punctures by removing large sticks and rubble, you needn't worry about creating a perfect seal. In the bottom of the liner, scatter a layer of medium-sized pebbles to a depth of approximately 2 inches. This underlayer allows surface water to drain to the catch-sheet below. Before you return the topsoil, enrich it with well-rotted manure, garden compost, or moistened peat moss. Then plant the bog

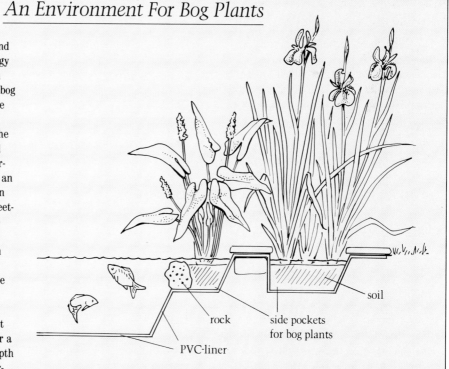

with some of the varied and delightful plants listed in the chapter, "Planting and Stocking Your Garden Pool."

The amount of watering required varies according to the weather. Try to keep the soil constantly moist by watering regularly during dry spells. Most bog plants are tough and will survive a few dry spells without extra watering, though they may not look their best.

Weeping cherry (*Prunus subhirtella* 'Pendula Plena')

Flowering dogwood (*Cornus florida*)

PLANTS FOR LANDSCAPING AROUND A WATER GARDEN

Scientific Name	Common Name	Hardiness Zone	Characteristics
TREES: Deciduous			
Acer palmatum 'Dissectum'	Cutleaf Japanese maple	6-8	6-12', rounded form, layered branches, deeply cut leaves, red fall color
Amelanchier spp.	Serviceberry	4-9	15-25', multistemmed, early white bloom, edible fruit, red fall color
Betula pendula cvs.	White birch	2-6	12-25', gracefully pyramidal with drooping limbs, white trunk bark
Cercis canadensis	Redbud	4-9	20-30', spreading crown, magenta early spring flowers, yellow fall color
Chionanthus virginicus	Fringe tree	3-9	12-30', may be wider than tall, outstanding white late spring flowers
Cornus florida	Flowering dogwood	5-8	20-30', layered branches, white or pink spring flowers, red fall fruit
Cornus kousa	Japanese dogwood	5-8	20-30', mottled trunk bark, white late spring flowers, red fall fruit
Cornus mas	Cornelian cherry	4-8	4-8', multistemmed, yellow early spring flowers, edible red fruit
Franklinia alatamaha	Franklin tree	5-8	20-25', slender form, fragrant white late summer flowers, red fall color
Metasequoia glyptostroboides	Dawn redwood	5-10	70-100' pyramidal deciduous conifer, soft needled leaves, reddish bark
Oxydendrum arboreum	Sourwood	5-9	25-30', pyramidal, white summer flowers, red to purple fall color
Prunus subhirtella 'Pendula'	Weeping Higan cherry	4-9	20-40', gracefully arching, slender twigs, pink spring flowers
Stewartia ovata	Mountain camellia	5-9	10-15', spreading branches, white summer flowers, red fall color
Styrax japonicus	Japanese snowbell	5-9	20-30', often wider than tall, white summer flowers, yellow fall color
TREES: Evergreen, including dwarf conifers			
Cedrus deodara	Deodar cedar	7-8	40-70', starts broadly pyramidal, becomes spreading, flat-topped
× *Cupressocyparis leylandii*	Leyland cypress	6-10	60-70', columnar to pyramidal form, good screen
Picea abies dwarf cvs.	Norway spruce	2-7	3-6', low, spreading, dense and compact forms, good accent plants
Pinus parviflora	Japanese white pine	4-7	25-50' graceful broad pyramid, picturesque
Pinus strobus dwarf cvs.	Eastern white pine	3-8	8-18', various forms, distinctive outlines, good accent plants
Pinus thunbergiana	Japanese black pine	5-7	20-80', broad irregular shape, use in a Japanese garden
Tsuga canadensis	Canada hemlock	3-7	40-80', graceful dark-green needled, good screen
Tsuga canadensis 'Pendula'	Sargent's weeping hemlock	3-7	6-8', broadly weeping form, wider than tall, makes a dense bush
SHRUBS: Deciduous			
Clethra alnifolia	Summer-sweet	3-9	3-8', fragrant, long-lasting, pink to white late summer flowers
Corylopsis glabrescens	Fragrant winter hazel	15-8	8-15', multistemmed, wide-spreading, yellow early spring flowers
Cytisus scoparius	Scotch or common broom	6-9	5-6', broad, upright or mounding forms, yellow, pink, red flowers
Enkianthus campanulatus	Redvein enkianthus	4-7	8-20', slender, upright; yellow spring flowers, red fall color
Euonymous alata	Burning bush	3-8	15-20', broad, flat-topped habit, red fall color, ridged branches
Fothergilla major	Large fothergilla	4-8	6-10', dense; fragrant white spring flowers, red fall color
Hamamelis spp.	Witch hazel	14-8	6-25', dense, spreading; yellow winter flowers, yellow fall color
Hypericum prolificum	Shrubby St.-John's-wort	3-8	1-4', dense, stiff stemmed; long-lasting yellow summer flowers
Ilex verticillata	Winterberry	3-9	6-10', densely branching, rounded form; red winter berries
Jasminum nudiflorum	Winter jasmine	6-10	3-4', spreading, trailing branches; yellow late winter flowers
Phyllostachys nigra	Black bamboo	8-10	4-15' thicket of leafy stems, stems turn black in second year
Potentilla fruticosa cvs.	Shrubby cinquefoil	2-7	1-4', bushy, slender stemmed, long-lasting yellow summer flowers

Azalea (*Rhododendron* hybrid)

Juniper (*Juniperus* species)

PLANTS FOR LANDSCAPING AROUND A WATER GARDEN

Scientific Name	Common Name	Hardiness Zone	Characteristics
SHRUBS: Evergreen			
Arctostaphlyos uva-ursi	Bearberry	6–8	6–12″ low dense groundcover, glossy leaves, red berries
Berberis thunbergii var. atropurpurea	Crimson pigmy barberry 'Crimson Pigmy'	4–8	1½–2′, bronze red foliage, small red winter berries
Buxis sempervirens	Boxwood	5–10	15–20′, dense, dark green foliage, slow growing, good trimmed formally
Chamaecyparis obtusa	Hinoki false cypress	3–8	3–12′, fan-shaped foliage, different forms, picturesque
Chamaecyparis pisifera 'Filifera'	Thread-branch false cypress	3–8	6–8′, mounded form; weeping, fine-textured twigs
Cotoneaster dammeri	Bearberry cotoneaster	5–10	½–2′, arching form, semievergreen, colorful red fall and winter fruit
Daphne odora	Winter daphne	4–7	4′, mounded and densely branched, pink to red late winter flowers
Euonymous fortunei cvs.	Winter creeper	4–8	4–6′ arching or climbing plant, some cultivars more shrubby
Ilex crenata 'Helleri'	Japanese Helleri holly	5–8	2–4′, dense, dark green leaves, mounding form, small black berries
Juniperus chinensis dwarf cvs.	Chinese juniper	2–9	sharp, needlelike foliage, pyramidal or creeping forms
Juniperus communis dwarf cvs.	Common juniper	2–9	varying dwarf forms, pyramidal to spreading, sharp needlelike foliage
Juniperus conferta dwarf cvs.	Shore juniper	2–9	low trailing groundcover, sharp needlelike foliage
Juniperus chinesis 'Procumbens'	Japanese garden juniper	4–9	8–12″, 4–5′ wide, low mounding plant, blue-green needlelike foliage
Juniperus horizontalis 'Wiltoni'	Blue rug juniper	4–9	4″, 8–10′ wide, dense mat of silver-blue needlelike foliage
Juniperus squamata cvs.	Singleseed juniper	4–9	various forms, prostrate to upright, blue-green needles
Leucothoe fontanesiana	Doghobble	4–6	2–4′, leathery, glossy, dark green leaves, spreading branches
Myrica pensylvanica	Bayberry	2–5	5–12′, semievergreen, upright dense form, persistent gray fruit
Nandina domestica 'Harbour Dwarf'	Dwarf heavenly bamboo	6–9	2–3′, compact, graceful form, red berries, red-tinged leaves in winter
Pieris japonica	Japanese andromeda	5–8	9–12′, upright, oval leaves, white early spring flowers
Rhododendron spp. and cvs.	Azalea	3–10	3–15′, various sizes and degrees of hardiness, showy spring flowers
Rhododendron spp. and cvs.	Rhododendron	5–10	1–10′, various sizes and degrees of hardiness, showy spring flowers
Taxus baccata 'Repandens'	Weeping English yew	6–9	2–4′ high, 12–15′ wide, dark green flexible needles, branches drooping
Yucca filamentosa	Adam's needle yucca	5–10	3–6′, stiff, swordlike leaves, spikes of creamy-white midsummer flowers

Japanese primrose (*Primula japonica*)

Candytuft (*Iberis sempervirens*)

PLANTS FOR LANDSCAPING AROUND A WATER GARDEN

Scientific Name	Common Name	Hardiness Zone	Characteristics
PERENNIALS			
Achillea spp.	Yarrow	3-9	3-5', lacy leaves, flat white, yellow or pink flowerheads in summer
Artemesia schmidtiana 'Silver Mound'	Silver mound	3-9	1' mounding plant with attractive silvery foliage
Aruncus dioicus	Goatsbeard	4-9	4-7' shrubby perennial, large compound leaves, white flower plumes
Asclepius tuberosa	Butterfly weed	3-61	½-3', long-lasting orange flowers in midsummer
Aster spp.	Hardy aster	3-9	1½-3', late summer to fall flowers, in white, blue, pink, lavender
Astilbe spp.	Spiraea	4-9	2' bushy mounds, lacy foliage, white, pink, or red summer flower plumes
Chrysanthemum spp. and cvs.	Chrysanthemum	5-9	1-4', fall flowers of various colors and forms
Coreopsis verticillata cvs.	Threadleaf coreopsis	4-10	1-3', delicate needlelike foliage, long-lasting yellow flowers in summer
Dicentra spectabilis	Bleeding-heart	2-8	2½', finely cut foliage, pendulous pink flowers in early spring
Echinacea purpurea	Purple coneflower	4-9	2-4' upright plant with bold purple midsummer to fall flowers
Gaillardia × *grandiflora*	Blanket flower	3-10	1-2', basal leaves; yellow, orange and red flowers all summer
Geranium spp.	Cranesbill	4-10	6"-3', mounding; spring or early summer flowers in pink, blues, white
Hemerocallis spp. and cvs.	Daylily	3-10	1½-3', with straplike leaves and lilylike flowers, many colors
Heuchera sanguinea cvs.	Coralbells	3-10	1-2½', with pink or red flowers on wiry stems, pretty basal leaves
Iberis sempervirens	Edging candytuft	5-9	1' evergreen clumps, white spring flowers, winter blooms in mild areas
Iris spp. and cvs.	Iris	5-9	1-4', swordlike leaves, late spring flowers, many colors
Liatris spicata	Gay feather	3-10	3', clumps of straplike leaves; narrow spikes of mauve or white flowers
Ligularia dentata cvs.	Ragwort	3-10	3-4', large, heart-shaped basal leaves; spikes of yellow flowers
Limonium latifolium	Sea lavender	3-9	2½', large glossy basal leaves, prolific flowers, blue, pink, white
Lythrum salicaria 'Morden's Pink'	Purple loosestrife	3-9	1½-5' upright plant, small, narrow leaves, pink midsummer to fall flower spikes
Miscanthus sinensis cvs.	Eulalia grass	5-9	3-8' upright grass, large graceful leaves, silky flower heads
Molina caerulea spp.	Moor grass	5-8	5-8' stiff upright grass, dense green or purple tufts, arching plumes
Ophiopogon japonicus	Mondo grass	7-10	6" grassy leaved clump, smaller than Liriope, light lilac flowers
Opuntia humifusa	Prickly pear cactus	6-10	3', spreading, 6" prickly pads, yellow flowers, rosy fruits
Paeonia spp. and cvs.	Peony	5-9	2-4', bushy, attractive foliage, fragrant spring flowers, many colors
Pennisetum alopecuroides	Fountain grass	5-9	2-4', slender bright-green with delicate silvery plumes
Polygonatum commutatum	Great Soloman's-seal	4-8	6', arching stems of rich green leaves, dainty spring flowers
Primula spp. and cvs.	Primrose	2-10	6"-4', spring flowers on stalks above basal leaves, many colors
Rodgersia aesculifolia	Rogersia	4-9	4', leaves like horse chestnut, large clusters of white summer flowers
Rudbeckia hirta	Black-eyed Susan	3-10	2-3' upright clumps; summer to fall flowers, yellow, dark brown centers
Salvia spp.	Sage	4-10	1½-4', with spikes of blue-purple, white, or pink flowers
Sedum spp.	Stonecrop	3-10	2"-2', succulent leaves, many forms, white, pink, yellow flowers
Tiarella cordifolia	Foamflower	4-8	1', leaves round, small white to reddish bell-shaped spring flowers
Tradescantia × *andersoniana*	Spiderwort	4-10	2' trailing plant; delicate summer flowers, white, pink, blue, purple
Veronica spp.	Speedwell	4-9	1-3', upright or trailing, spikes of small summer flowers, many colors

Japanese iris (*Iris kaempferi*)

Plantain lily (*Hosta undulata*)

Lilyturf (*Liriope muscari* 'Variegata')

Lady fern (*Athyrium filix-femina*)

PLANTS FOR LANDSCAPING AROUND A WATER GARDEN

Scientific Name	Common Name	Hardiness Zone	Characteristics
GROUNDCOVERS			
Ajuga reptans	Carpet bugleweed	4–10	6–10″, thick mat of oval leaves, spring flower spikes, blue, pink, white
Asarum canadense	Snakeroot, wild ginger	4–8	1′ deciduous groundcover, large heart-shaped leaves
Athyrium spp.	Japanese painted fern	2–8	4′, slightly drooping fronds, attractive white markings
Calluna vulgaris	Scotch heather	4–6	6″–2′, tiny leaves, small white, pink, or purple flowers, summer or fall
Ceratostigma plumbaginoides	Blue plumbago	5–9	1½′, blue flowers, summer into fall, foliage red-tinged in fall
Dryopteris spp.	Wood fern	2–8	4′, arching delicate fronds
Epimedium spp.	Bishop's hat	4–9	1′, graceful foliage, wiry stems, delicate flowers
Festuca ovina glauca	Blue fescue	4–9	6″ spiky mounds of blue-green tufts
Galium odoratum	Sweet woodruff	4–9	6″–1′, small whorled leaves, tiny white spring flowers
Hedera helix	English ivy	6–9	clinging vine, fast spreading, evergreen foliage, some variegated
Hosta spp. and cvs.	Plantain lily	3–9	1–3′, decorative, often variegated, basal leaves, late summer flowers
Liriope muscari	Lilyturf	6–10	1′ semievergreen grassy leaved clumps, small lilac to purple flowers
Osmunda cinnamomea	Cinnamon fern	5–8	5′, long, broad fronds, dramatic clumps
Osmunda regalis	Royal fern	5–8	4–6′, graceful upright fronds
Thymus spp.	Thyme	5–9	2″ creeper, aromatic leaves, purplish or white late spring flowers

Right: A low stone bridge enhances the brick and rock used in the landscape of this pool.
Below: A traditional arched bridge adds color, interest, and a beautiful vantage point to the subtle grace of a Japanese-style garden.

BRIDGES AND STEPPING STONES

For a large pool or water garden, a bridge is the crowning touch. It also has practical purposes in providing a convenient footpath across the water and a viewing area for observing the aquatic plants and water life.

Whether or not your water garden is sizable enough to accommodate a bridge is a matter of judgment. For example, an arched bridge with handrails would overwhelm a small lily pond, but a stone slab spanning the narrowest part of the pool may be the perfect touch.

The photographs on these pages will give you an idea of the small footbridges that can be built over garden ponds. For many gardens, the most suitable bridge will have straight, simple lines and be set close to the water. Unless children's safety is a factor, conspicuous handrails aren't necessary.

The color, style, and material of a bridge should be in keeping with the architectural style of your house and the other features of your garden. Match a redwood bridge to a redwood garden bench. Echo the stones edging a pool with a stone-slab bridge. Complement a white-trimmed house with a wooden bridge painted white.

Installing Stepping Stones

Even a small pond can hold a few stepping stones that form a simple pathway from shore to shore. Flat-topped boulders of native stone

Right: Wooden steps topped with stone span this narrow stream meandering through a garden of summer flowers. Below: The rugged mass of these bold stepping-stones contrasts wonderfully with the clean lines of the pool.

make an excellent choice. However, stones should not be placed directly on the bottom of the pool lest they puncture the liner when you lift or move them. Instead, set them on cinder blocks, which are smooth enough to leave the liner unharmed. Cinder blocks will not show once the pool has aged. Mortar may also be used as a footing for stepping stones, but treat it for excessive alkalinity (see page 29).

Your choice of materials and placement of stepping stones should agree with the formal or informal design of your garden. Square or round stepping stones are best suited to the formal pond. Informal water gardens are better served with stepping stones of rough-hewn, natural shapes.

Placement is important, both for walking and for viewing. If you space the stones irregularly or on a slight curve, the viewer must walk slowly when crossing. As a practical matter, the stones should be kept dry. If they are splashed with water or shaded, slippery algae may grow on them, so keep them away from a fountain or waterfall. Use a wire brush whenever necessary to remove algae.

When planning the layout for stepping stones, test your design on graph paper to make sure that there is enough room in your pool. The location of the stones may influence your placement of water lilies and marginal plants. Conversely, built-in marginal shelves may interfere with your arrangement of the stepping stones.

Building a Wooden Bridge

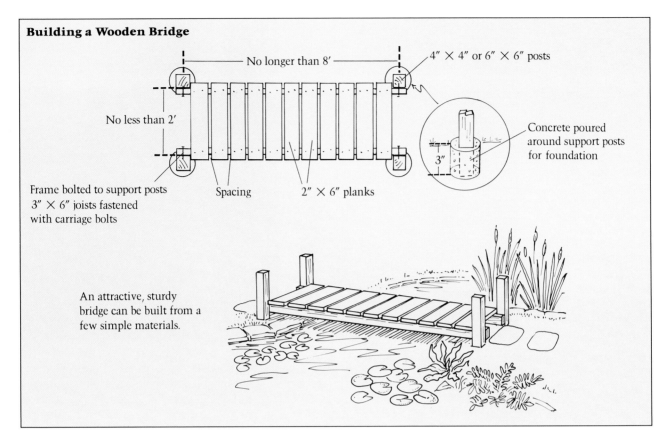

No longer than 8'

4″ × 4″ or 6″ × 6″ posts

No less than 2'

Concrete poured around support posts for foundation

3″

Frame bolted to support posts 3″ × 6″ joists fastened with carriage bolts

Spacing

2″ × 6″ planks

An attractive, sturdy bridge can be built from a few simple materials.

Installing a Wooden Bridge

A plank bridge is the most practical and versatile type of bridge for an informal water garden. Cedar or pressure-treated lumber is preferable and will have a life span of between 10 and 15 years. Other kinds of wood can be treated with preservative, but be sure to read the label carefully, since some preservatives can be harmful to plant and aquatic life. Oak, elm, and similar hardwoods withstand water damage better than do softwoods such as pine.

A comfortable width for walking is 24 inches. However, by making the bridge wider, you can accommodate a garden cart or lawn mower. Use lengthwise or crosswise planks measuring 2 inches by 6 inches, 2 inches by 8 inches, or 2 inches by 12 inches, and leave some spacing between the planks to allow rainwater to drain off and air to flow through.

Support posts should never penetrate the pool liner. If you have a long span, use bricks or concrete blocks under the center. These center supports should be cushioned by an extra layer of scrap PVC or rubber matting so that they do not rest directly on the liner. The span between supports should be no more than 8 feet.

Supporting posts at each end of the bridge should be a minimum of 4 inches by 4 inches—preferably 6 inches by 6 inches—thick and mounted in 3-foot-deep post holes. If your soil is very sandy or crumbly, pour a concrete foundation and hide the concrete surface with soil. Fasten 3 by 6 joists crosswise to the posts with carriage bolts. Mount the planks on this frame with galvanized nails or brass screws.

For a very large pond where several spans are needed to cross the water, consider placing the sections at angles to one another to describe a zigzag pathway. For one short span, you might make a wooden bridge that arches upward in the center, as in Japanese designs.

Handrails should be sturdy and functional. The top rail should be at least 2 inches by 2 inches or made of a 3-inch-diameter pole, at a height of no less than 39 inches, and smoothly finished so that there are no splinters. If the railings are made of softwood, make sure they are protected with a nontoxic preservative. For the safety of children, you may want to stretch dark nylon netting between the supporting beams. This netting is almost invisible from a distance.

The romantic appearance of this white latticework bridge fits gracefully into a country setting.

In perfect keeping with the natural look of this garden, a wood-chip path leads visitors on a meandering walk around the pond.

Installing a Bridge Over a Culvert Pipe

Over a small waterfall or streambed, a single concrete or stone slab creates a permanent-looking footpath. The slab should have concrete footings on either bank. Gravel, pebbles, or small rocks can be placed around the footings to hide the concrete. When working with any kind of concrete, cinder blocks, or bricks, remember to treat it thoroughly to leach out the lime after the mortar has set. If the pond water becomes excessively alkaline, it will kill any fish.

You can also direct a stream feeding a pool through a culvert pipe to create a bridge and a path. Cover the pipe with concrete or soil topped with grass, gravel, or brick to create a gentle arch.

DESIGNING PATHS AND SEATING AREAS

As you are planning the landscaping, decide where you would like your visitors to sit, stroll, or dine, so the placement of these areas is not left to chance. A path leading to a bench where you can sit and enjoy the water lilies makes a charming addition to a garden. Plan other areas for dining, viewing, or exclusively for gardening. Be sure also to give yourself easy access to the pool for maintenance. For

Left: The concrete bench echoes the concrete edges of the pool, creating a harmonious setting for quiet reflection. Right: Shaded by overhanging branches, this expansive brick patio provides a cool spot to relax and contemplate the garden scene.

instance, you might want a flat rock to kneel on when reaching for the pump.

If there will be foot traffic from one place to another, the path should probably be paved. The approach to a bridge can be finished in a number of ways. A gravel or pebble path makes an attractive approach to a wooden bridge, as does a plank walkway. You can also arrange irregular flat stones or crazy paving to make an informal walkway to the bridge.

Brick, bluestone, or square blocks are sometimes used for a formal path and are in keeping with a stone-slab bridge. In a woodland setting, a path of shredded bark looks quite handsome. When laying out paths try to create gentle curves, which are easy to follow, rather than sharp turns. Paths should link the most direct routes from house and patio to pond, while still being attractively shaped. If the path does not make a direct link, viewers may be tempted to take a shortcut and your lawn may get worn.

Alongside a water garden is a perfect place to relax with friends, share a good meal, or sit quietly enjoying the birds and scenery and the gentle splash of a waterfall or fountain. In fact, a well-planned seating area may be the key to gaining the most pleasure from your garden pool. Choose a simple wooden or stone bench in keeping with the materials used in the rest of the landscape.

Choosing Patio Design and Size

Although the construction of a patio, terrace, or deck is an ambitious undertaking, the results can be satisfying. A seating area should provide a comfortable amount of space for your outdoor activities, while not blocking the view of the garden. A terrace or patio next to a pool should have ample room for strolling, and a wide area specifically for sitting and dining. Seating should be located where you will not get too much glare from sun reflecting on water. The best viewing areas are generally situated toward the south end, where the sun will be behind you when you are seated.

A deck or terrace overhanging the water's edge is attractive for a large pond, but will overwhelm the proportions of a small pool. Since the water becomes a natural focal point, you should not hide it behind large terrace structures such as a permanent outdoor grill or wooden benches. For a small pool, the deck or terrace is best placed at pool level. Leave sight lines open for viewing the plants, aquatic life and other landscape features.

Selecting Building Materials

Many attractive materials are available for patios and decks. The main thing to consider is whether you can do the work yourself or wish to use the services of a mason, bricklayer, carpenter, or landscape contractor.

A flagstone patio running the length of the pool provides ample room for entertaining.

must be evenly spaced. Around the curve of a formal pool or garden bed, cut the paving to fit the radius exactly. Use spacing pegs to maintain the distance between paving units. (For more information, see Ortho's *Basic Masonry Techniques.*)

Installing a Wooden Deck

A permanent, raised wooden deck can be installed on firm, stable ground, and requires little landscaping or excavation. Support the deck on 6-inch by 6-inch wooden posts, with 3-inch by 4-inch or 4-inch by 6-inch bearer beams. For greatest strength, the posts should be mounted on a reinforcing bar that is embedded in a 12-inch by 12-inch concrete footing. Decking planks can be laid in straight, parallel courses or in a diagonal zigzag pattern. (For more information on patios and decks, consult Ortho's *How to Design & Build Decks & Patios.*)

GARDEN LIGHTING

Light cast on a water garden at night creates magical, dramatic effects. Underwater lights transform falling water into an abundant white cascade with the power to mesmerize. With well-planned spotlights, you can create perpetual moonlight so that the still water of a garden pond becomes a reflective pool mirroring branches, flowers, and foliage.

Designing Lighting

It is more effective to spotlight a few well-chosen areas than to floodlight an entire garden. High-intensity general lighting is better left to the football field. A few well-placed lights seem to make the entire garden glow, even though the lights only touch selected plants and garden features. Spotlights and area lights can be artfully positioned so that they emphasize contours and landscape features, without lighting up the entire yard.

There are four basic kinds of lighting to consider for specific garden effects: underwater lighting, mirror lighting, spotlighting, and accent lighting. Underwater lighting has perhaps the most limited use in a water garden. Though they would seem an obvious choice for a pool, underwater lights can bring out the worst rather than the best in your water garden by creating too much glare and illuminating the silt and debris. They also eliminate

Brick, tile, or stone must be constructed correctly and built on the proper underlayer or foundation. The patio area must be designed so that it drains efficiently. Walking areas should be comfortable underfoot, and paving must be secure.

In choosing materials for the area, consider the visual impact of texture and color. A redwood deck may complement a ranch-style house with dark shingles, but it might be out of place next to a brick colonial house. Traditional materials such as cut stone, weathered brick, and crazy paving fit in with a naturalistic landscape. Wooden decks, square bluestone pavers, and quarry tiles have sharp, clean-cut lines and textures, giving a more contemporary appearance.

Laying Paving

All paving must be laid on a solid, level base. Crumbly or boggy soil in the area must be excavated and replaced before paving work can begin. You can install a subsurface drain to carry water away. In cold climates the excavation usually has a 3- to 6-inch layer of compacted rubble on top of compacted soil, covered by 2 to 3 inches of sand; in warm climates all that is needed is a 4-inch base of compacted sand. A layer of smooth cement is poured on top of this foundation. For the best appearance, regularly shaped paving units reflections, so you lose the romantic mirror effect of a pond at night. Underwater lights are best where the water is very clear, as it is in a swimming pool. Submerged spotlights can be very effective in illuminating a specimen water lily or lotus. When directed upward through the white water of a bubbling fountain or waterfall, an underwater spotlight casts a radiant gleam. Whenever used, such lights should be directed away from, not toward, the viewer.

Mirror lighting is effective for tall specimen and border plants. Hidden lights shine upward into the foliage of trees, shrubs, or flowers near the pond, while the water stays dark. To a viewer standing on the far side, the uplit plant is perfectly mirrored in the dark pool, the reflection changing with each ripple in the water surface.

Accent lighting creates striking displays with selective, low-level illumination. Ferns, grasses, broad-leaved plants, and rock garden features can be lit from the front and highlighted by concealed lights that are dim or medium-bright. These gentle accents add a new dimension to the landscape and emphasize the beauty of garden features and foliage.

You may want to install attractive utility lights around a water garden to light up pathways, terraces, and steps. This is especially necessary for safety reasons near the edge of a terrace that overhangs an unlit pond. Although utility lighting is functional, the fixtures should be placed where they are as inconspicuous as possible. Often, knee- or ankle-level lights are used around a path to provide lighting that is safe without being bright. If you install general area lighting, place the lamps well above head level so that they do not shine into the eyes of people who are standing or seated.

Installing Garden Lighting
Outdoor electrical fixtures must conform to local regulations, and a number of precautions should be observed when working with outdoor cable, conduit, and connectors. If your local codes permit, you can do the work yourself but there is some danger in working with lights and electrical equipment that is to be exposed to water and weather. It is recommended that the installation of underwater

lights be done by a licensed electrician. (For more information on lighting, see Ortho's *How to Design & Install Outdoor Lighting.*)

For safety, all exterior wiring should be fitted with a ground fault circuit interrupter (GFCI), which can be installed in an outlet box by an electrician. The GFCI cuts off the power automatically whenever there is danger of a short circuit or overload. All fittings on outdoor connections, spotlights, and floodlights should have weatherproof moldings, rubberized cables, and sealed gaskets. Additional requirements for types of cable and installation may be specified in local building codes, so be sure to check local ordinances.

There are two basic lighting systems from which to choose, a low-voltage (12-volt) system and a standard-voltage (120-volt) system. The low-voltage system is safer, easier to install, easily rearranged, and less expensive. But it cannot operate high-intensity spotlights or floodlights. For this reason, it is better suited to a small garden. A standard-voltage system can sustain brilliant lighting over large areas, but you'll need it only to illuminate a large garden or uplight full-sized trees. For either system, all fixtures, connectors, cable, and conduit should be of the best quality to ensure reliability and safety.

A low-voltage set includes a combination transformer and optional time clock. The transformer is connected to the 120-volt source of power. (The power source should be installed by a licensed electrician.) Once the transformer is plugged in, you will be working with only 12 volts of power, which is quite safe. Cable can be lightly covered with turf or soil, and fixtures are easily moved.

A 120-volt system must conform to the electrical code and must be inspected before being connected. All wiring should pass through long-lasting, aluminum alloy or PVC conduit, which has to be buried in trenches. Since the conduit must be moved if a fixture is relocated, standard-voltage fixtures should be considered permanent.

Camouflaging the Light Fixtures
Electrical equipment can be unsightly and should be concealed to preserve the appearance of your garden. Cable and conduit can be buried, but outlet boxes and transformers must be mounted above ground. These may be

Creating soft reflections of a moonlit night, mirror lighting transforms this garden pool into a romantic tropical setting.

Lit from beneath, the lily pads make dark silhouettes against the bright water, creating intricate patterns of light and dark.

A light concealed at the base of this redwood tree illuminates the trunk, creating a mirrorlike image in the pool.

concealed behind the far side of a tree, post, or heavily foliaged plant. If you run a cable up a tree, use plastic clips to hold it in place.

Selecting Fixtures and Lamps

Standard spotlights and floodlights are mounted in basic can-type fixtures. These are usually dark colored but unattractive, so they should be concealed. You can buy attractive, well-designed fixtures that are unobtrusive or ornamental in the daytime. Darker finishes, such as black enamel or weathered brass, are less distracting than white or shiny brass. Many custom-designed and handcrafted lamps and lamp holders are available from specialty garden catalogs, but be selective in choosing a style that blends with your garden.

Spotlights, floodlights, and general area lights vary in intensity, color, and efficiency. The most commonly used bulb for outdoor spotlighting and floodlighting is a PAR lamp (parabolic aluminized reflector), which comes in high-voltage and low-voltage versions and resembles a car headlight. Similar kinds of spotlights, designated R (for reflector) and ER (for elliptical reflector) are also available in various wattages. These lamps provide incandescent light, which is the most natural-looking illumination for a garden.

High-intensity discharge lamps are also available. These include mercury vapor, high-pressure sodium, and metal halide lamps. Mercury vapor lamps give off a strong blue light; metal halide lamps have a slight greenish tinge and high-pressure sodium lights give off a yellowish light. These high-intensity lamps can produce bold, stark, moonlit effects that can feel eerie. Low-wattage incandescent lamps are warmer and more inviting since their light spectrum concentrates on the warm reds and yellows. At high wattages, normal incandescent lights and quartz incandescent lamps produce a whiter light, but one that is still warmer than that produced by high-intensity discharge lamps.

Wonderland effects can be achieved by using colored filters on lights, but test the colors at night to make sure that you like them. Some colors are best avoided. Yellow and amber light make plants look bleached; red looks unnatural and hot. Pale pink complements natural complexions and white marble statuary, but is not attractive on plant foliage.

Caring for Your Garden Pool

A few minutes every week is all the time it takes to keep your pool in good health.

As a garden pool goes through seasonal cycles, you'll need to carry out some routine chores to help maintain the good health and appearance of plants and aquatic life. Often, maintenance is the key to preventing future problems. But seasonal chores can be kept to a minimum if your pond has healthy, well-balanced aquatic life.

Each part of the year brings changes to the water garden. In spring, before surface plants spread their leaves, algae may be a problem. In summer, typical problems may be water evaporation, rampant growth, and plant pests. When the weather is extremely hot, the level of the pool may go down as much as an inch a week. Some water will have to be added regularly to keep the pool full. Don't wait until the level is very low, or the plants, fish, and the pool liner may be injured. Garden beds may need regular weeding and the aquatic plants may need thinning or dividing. You may want to clean the filter approximately once a week to ensure the clearest water.

In autumn you should prevent buildup of decaying leaves on the bottom of the pool. For winter there are a few preparations to be made. The pool may have to be drained and the liner cleaned. Tender plants should be removed for protective storage (see page 106). Hardy plants should be pruned and divided. You may also want to remove the pump for cleaning and storage.

During winter, an area of the pool's surface needs to be kept free from ice so that fish will not be poisoned by the gases that build up from decaying organic matter and their own respiration. Since fish feed only minimally in winter, no further attention is necessary unless the pond threatens to freeze over.

Scooping out occasional tree leaves before they sink to the bottom of the pond helps keep the water fresh.

Right: In an established pool, the leaves of aquatic plants spread across the surface and shade the water, discouraging excess algal growth.
Below: Single-celled algae cloud this newly stocked pool. Once the nutrients dissolved in the water are used up, the annoying algae will die.

ALGAE

Algae represent one of the foremost concerns of beginning water gardeners. When a pool is first installed, the growth of abundant single-celled algae can cause the water to look like pea soup because the aquatic plants haven't established themselves enough to shade the water; algae thrive in the sunlight. This situation is temporary, so don't be alarmed. Similarly, when the seasons change, the water may become temporarily clouded with algae if the pool gets out of ecological balance. In spring, algal growth takes off before that of other aquatic plants, which don't begin to grow until the water warms up. Over winter, fish may have nibbled submerged plants down to tufts, which cannot produce shade. But after the water lily leaves spread across the surface and submerged plants are reestablished, their foliage sufficiently shades the water to kill excessive algae. The algae will die and sink to the bottom almost overnight once a critical point has been reached in the ecology of the pond.

As fish begin feeding off the algae and the submerged plants compete for dissolved nutrients, the cloudy green color gradually disappears. The time required for this transformation varies with every pond and depends on numerous factors such as weather, water chemistry, and the number of plants.

Algae flourish whenever they have an ample supply of nutrients, minerals, carbon dioxide, warm water, and sunlight. Decayed fish food, fertilizer, and mineral salts that occur naturally in fresh water provide their nourishment. Any activity that stirs up nutrient sediment from the bottom will have the effect of feeding algae and helping them grow. Therefore, avoid runoff from highly fertilized lawns or gardens, and never stir up the bottom unnecessarily during the growing season.

The best control for algae is good ecology—maintaining an adequate balance of surface and marginal plants, submerged plants, and fish. It may require some experimentation to achieve the right balance. Further controls can be implemented, if necessary, with algaecides or by filtering.

Algaecides

An algaecide is a chemical formulation that kills existing algae in the water, but does not prevent more from growing. Therefore, it is only a temporary solution. One algaecide made specifically for garden ponds causes the suspended particles of algae to sink to the bottom of the pool, from where they will then have to be removed with a pool sweep.

At the highest concentrations, algaecides may harm fish or plant life. One formulation is safe for plants but deadly to fish. An algaecide sold in aquarium stores and labeled "safe for goldfish ponds," is safe for fish but not for plants. It is essential to read all the labels carefully and use the proper concentrations of any algaecide.

In fountains or pools where you aren't growing plants or fish, algaecides or swimming pool chemicals will keep the water crystal clear. Their routine use isn't recommended for a water garden, however.

Dye

To create a dramatic reflective surface and to camouflage algae, you can dye the water black. This won't harm aquatic plants or fish, but slows algae growth by reducing sunlight. Use ¼ cup of black powdered artist's pigment, called nigrosine, for every 1,000 gallons of water. Apply once a month or as needed.

The darkened water is highly reflective, mirroring water lily blossoms and tall border plants and trees. The pool looks deeper than it really is and becomes a dramatic and mysterious focal point.

Filtering

Water can also be kept clear if it is filtered. Attached to the intake of the pump, the filter removes fish wastes, sediment, and algae, which cloud the water. Like algaecides, a filter does not alter the basic conditions that encourage algae growth.

There are two types of filters, mechanical and biological. The mechanical types are most commonly used in garden pools. They work by forcing the water through a filter pad or screen that traps the debris.

The biological filter at the rear of this pool keeps the water clear by relying on bacteria to consume debris and excess algae.

Above: The filter pad of this mechanical filter wraps around a cylinder. It should be removed for cleaning. Below: Several times a month, hose off particles and algae that may clog the filter; catch the dirty water in a bucket to prevent it from reentering the pool.

pressure to feed the fountain (which slows down the pump) as well as circulate the water at least once every two hours. (See pages 31 to 34 for more information on pumps.)

Biological filters rely on bacteria to consume the suspended matter and dissolved nutrients. Water is forced through a large container of gravel or rocks on which the bacteria grow. A biological filter requires slower water recirculation then does a mechanical filter. The pool water should be recirculated once every four or five hours.

Water Treatment

You may need to occasionally drain the water from the pool for a thorough cleaning, and you'll need to regularly replace water lost through evaporation. Whenever fresh water is introduced in large quantities, precautions should be taken to ensure that chlorine compounds will not harm the fish. When replacing all the water in the pool, use a purifying agent to eliminate chlorine compounds so that you can return the fish as soon as possible (see pages 28, 70, and 101). Do not reintroduce fish or plants until the water is at the same temperature as it was before being drained. If you wish to speed this process, you can blend hot water into the pool to warm it up before you add the dechlorinating agent.

Algae flourish in mineral-laden fresh water, so be prepared for renewed growth whenever you clean and refill the pool. In dry summer months when there is a continuous water loss through evaporation, it is best to top up the pool every few days rather than top it up in large doses so that algae bloom won't be a problem. When you top up the pool by an inch or less, the standing water dilutes the new water so that you can fill the pool directly from your garden hose without treating it for chlorine.

A number of different kinds of mechanical filters, with screens and filter pads of varying sizes are available from mail-order water garden suppliers and aquatic plant nurseries. You can reuse the filter pads many times, but they must be regularly cleaned for the filtering process to be effective. A weekly rinsing of the filter pad is recommended. Rinsing more often, even daily, produces the clearest water, but is not usually necessary.

A mechanical filter pump with the capacity to circulate half the water in the pool every hour is the right size. For instance, a pool holding 400 gallons requires a filter pump with a capacity of 200 gallons per hour (GPH).

If you connect a piece of tubing to the outlet, you can operate a fountain or waterfall from the same pump. However, the pump must have the capacity to produce enough

CONTROLLING MOSQUITOES

Although most people consider still water to be a breeding place for mosquitoes, a pond stocked with goldfish, golden orfes, or mosquito fish (*Gambusia*) has built-in mosquito control. When these active fish feed, their first choice is mosquito larvae. A properly balanced and well-stocked pool shouldn't be a source of pesky mosquitoes.

DRAINING AND CLEANING A POOL

A balanced pond may go for 10 years or more without ever needing to be cleaned, but sometimes a thorough draining may be necessary. If the water has become polluted by runoff containing weed killer or herbicides, all plants must be removed and the water changed immediately. In some areas, an annual cleaning is desirable to remove leaves, sediment and excess algae. Another reason for draining a pond is to find and repair a leak.

Fall is the best time for cleaning a pond. During that time the fish are less active and the aquatic plants are dormant, so they will suffer less stress when moved. Fall is also the best time to remove any dead leaves that have settled to the bottom, so they won't decompose over the winter and rob the oxygen supply in the pool. Cleaning in early spring, however, provides a good opportunity to divide and transplant aquatic plants.

If you have a drainage area lower than the pond level, siphon off the pool water through a tube. Be sure to hold a net or strainer over the end of the tube that is in the water so that no fish or debris get sucked down. If siphoning is not possible, you can pump out the water with a submerged pump. However, be sure the pump does not run dry, which may cause the motor to burn out.

It is impractical to try netting fish out of a full pond. Instead, drain the pool until the water is only about 6 inches deep before you attempt to catch the fish. If the water level is too low, the fish may be injured by their own gaseous wastes.

The bottom of the pool will have to be emptied in bucketfuls, by hand, after the fish and plants have been removed. Clean the empty pool with a stiff plastic brush, which won't puncture the liner, rinsing as you go. The only cleanser you should use is elbow grease. Refill the pool as soon as possible, then treat the fresh water with a dechlorinator, if needed (see page 28).

Fish Care During Cleaning

Whenever you disturb the water in a pool, you are likely to stir up sediment from the bottom. For this reason, it is best to fill holding tubs, such as large, clean, garbage pails, with pond water and set them aside in the shade for the fish before you begin cleaning the pool. Add a few submerged plants to the pail to provide the fish with oxygen. On the average, you

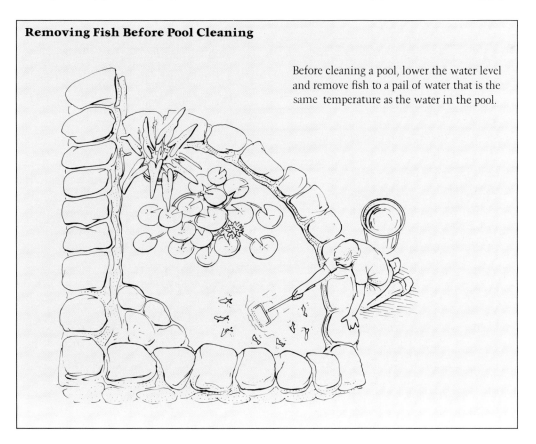

Removing Fish Before Pool Cleaning

Before cleaning a pool, lower the water level and remove fish to a pail of water that is the same temperature as the water in the pool.

Before releasing fish into your pool, float them in a plastic bag of water from their holding container. Keep the bag shaded, so the fish adjust to the temperature of the pool.

should allow 1 gallon of water for every 1 inch of fish. If the individual fish are more than 4 inches long, you need to aerate the water with a fish tank bubbler.

You can corral the fish with a net and then net and move them to the holding container. Snails, mussels, and clams should also be removed from the last few inches of water and placed in the same container as the fish.

To prevent the fish from being shocked, do not return them directly to the pool if the temperature of the water in the holding container differs by more than 5° F from that of the pool. Instead, place them in a plastic bag of water taken from the holding container. Float the bag in the shade on the pool surface. If no shade is available, cover the bag with a cloth. This will help the fish adjust to the temperature of the pool water. After about 20 minutes, gently release the fish into the pool.

If you keep them in the holding tub or plastic bag too long, ammonia may build up in the water from fish wastes and stress.

Add back several buckets of the original pond water to the pool. This will inoculate the freshly cleaned pool with necessary microorganisms.

Plant Care During Cleaning

After you have begun draining the pool, remove the tubs of plants. Wrap them in wet newspaper, cover with a plastic garbage bag, and place them in the shade. Place submerged plants and other small floating plants in a bucket of pond water. Submerged aquatic plants will be unable to recover if exposed to the air and allowed to dry out. In cold climates, if you drain and clean a pond in the fall, wait until after the first killing frost. Then remove all the leaves and stems from water lilies, lotus, and surface plants. Hardy plants can be returned to the pool; the roots of tender plants should be taken indoors for storage (see pages 104 and 106).

REPAIRING LEAKS

If you are trying to find a leak in your garden pool, let the water trickle out until the level remains constant. This tells you that the leak is probably somewhere at that level. You can easily repair leaks in PVC or fiberglass by using a patching kit obtainable from your water-garden supplier. All surfaces must be clean and dry before you begin patching. Concrete pools can also be repaired, either by plugging the cracks or by installing a flexible liner shaped to fit the concrete shell. A concrete shell can be plugged when the pool is full or empty, depending upon the compound used. It must be drained and dried before being lined with PVC.

Patching PVC Liner

Patches for PVC are applied with the same adhesive that is used to seal the seams of liners. When patched properly, the bonding material is unlikely to open up again during the life of the pool. Be sure to use only PVC adhesive made specifically for flexible materials. (The kind carried by most hardware stores is for the repair of rigid PVC pipe and is unsuitable for thin, flexible liners.)

Before repairing, find out what caused the tear or puncture in the first place. Remove any rubble or sharp objects underneath the liner and add fresh sand beneath the liner if necessary. Otherwise, the leak will be reopened by the sharp object.

After you have cleaned and dried the liner around the leak, apply PVC adhesive to the area and to the PVC patch. (Trimmings from the edge of the PVC make good patching material.) Both surfaces need to set for about two minutes to become sticky. Then place the patch over the leak and apply pressure. Usually, the pool can be refilled in an hour. Read the adhesive label for specific instructions.

Repairing PVC Liner

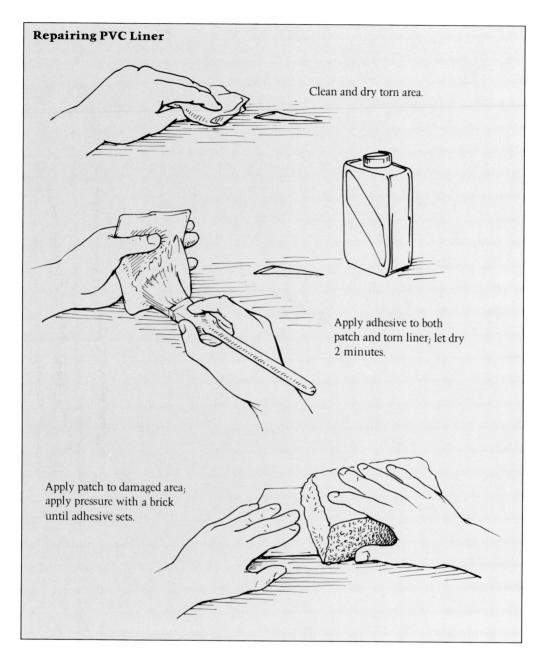

Clean and dry torn area.

Apply adhesive to both patch and torn liner; let dry 2 minutes.

Apply patch to damaged area; apply pressure with a brick until adhesive sets.

Patching Fiberglass

Since fiberglass is highly durable, any crack or hole in the bottom of a prefabricated pool indicates that the base is uneven or that stones are protruding underneath the liner. Unless you can find the cause, the leak is likely to recur. If necessary, remove the shell after it has been drained and check the base for dips, bumps, or sharp stones. Correct these before replacing the shell.

Any fiberglass repair kit is suitable for a fiberglass pool—many kits are available for repairing fiberglass boats or for cosmetic work on damaged cars. Read the label to make sure the quantity of woven mesh included in the kit is large enough to cover the entire area that needs patching. Instructions for patching are detailed on the box. With a piece of sandpaper, roughen up the area around the leak so that the resin will bond tightly to the shell. A resin and a catalyst come in separate tubes or containers. Mix the two in the correct proportions and then spread the mixture on the fiberglass mat. Lay the resin-soaked mat over the crack or hole so that it covers and seals the leak. Once the fiberglass mat has set, it will be as strong as the surrounding material.

Repairing Concrete

Whether new or old, a concrete pool may crack as a result of flaws in construction, extreme shifts in soil, or an invasion of aggressive tree roots. A temporary remedy for small cracks is a quick-setting cement that can be applied under water. It hardens in three minutes and forms a durable, waterproof bond. Other types of sealer are available to fix hairline cracks.

If the cracking is severe, the best solution may be to line the entire pool with a flexible liner. (Follow steps 2, 6, and 7 on pages 23 to 26.) Before installing PVC or butyl rubber, examine the concrete, fill deep indentations and smooth out rough spots so that the liner will not be punctured. You'll need to camouflage the edge of the liner, which often means removing the coping and reinstalling it over the edge of the liner. Once in place, the liner will not leak even if new cracks open up in the concrete.

DIVIDING AQUATIC PLANTS

Hardy water lilies can be propagated by root division. The root section of the water lily is a rhizome, usually a long woody underground stem that sends out roots from the bottom and growing points from the top and sides. By dividing sections of rootstock that have growing points, you can start new plants each season or when the container becomes overcrowded.

To divide the plants, dig up the rootstock and wash it off. It may be shaped like a sweet potato, a stick, or a small pineapple and may be soft or hard. Find the growing points. Active growing points will have leaves of various sizes, depending upon their maturity, sprouting from them; dormant points look like buds or potato eyes. Separate the rootstocks into pieces containing one or two plantlets or buds. You can break soft rootstocks, but tough rhizomes will need to be cut or sawed into chunks. Then plant the new rootstocks in separate containers with fresh soil and fertilizer. Hardy water lilies can be divided at any time during the growing season, which is usually from late April to early October. However, most gardeners prefer to divide them in the spring, rather than disturb the leaves and blossoms by digging up the rootstock in midseason.

Even if you don't want to start new plants, you should divide the rootstock every three or four years to prevent overcrowding. Plants from new rootstock are more vigorous and produce more blossoms. If the foliage of an old plant begins to look sickly, it may be a sign that the rootstock should be divided.

Lotus can be propagated in the same way. The lotus tuber is long and thin, with slim growing tips branching off the main part of the tuber. Divide the tubers in spring and plant each section in fresh soil.

Tropical water lilies do not have rhizomes. In fall they may form storage tubers just below the soil level. These can be propagated after a frost has nipped the foliage. Insert your fingers just below the crown and feel for the 1- to 2-inch-long egg-shaped tubers. Pull these from the soil and wash them clean. In frost-free areas, pot these up separately. In cold climates, store the tubers in moist sand in a closed glass jar kept at 45° F over the winter. If water is visible in the bottom of the jar, it is too wet. Replant in spring.

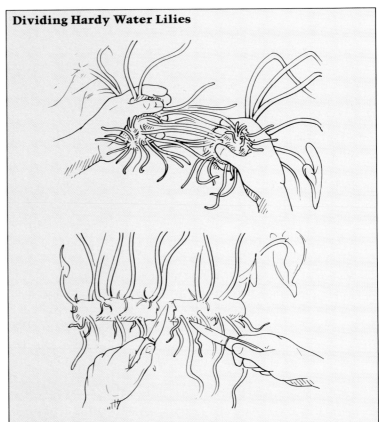

Dividing Hardy Water Lilies

If the rootstock is soft and shaped somewhat like a pineapple, it can be divided by tearing the roots apart. Be sure each division contains one or more growing points (above). Cut tough sticklike rhizomes into divisions with a knife or pruning saw (below).

Bog and marginal plants need division when their containers become crowded. The best time to divide is in early spring just when growth is beginning, though aquatics may be divided at any time up to a month before the first frost in fall. Iris plants are best divided in the fall.

Each type of plant requires a slightly different technique, depending upon the type of roots it has. Use your experience with other garden plants to guide you. You may need to saw a tangled root ball apart, separating the individual plants. Or, if the plant has rhizomes, cut them into separate rootstocks as you would a hardy water lily. Plant up all the divisions in separate containers, or discard the weakest ones and replant only the strongest.

AUTUMN AND WINTER CARE IN COLD CLIMATES

In cold climate areas, you will need to prevent autumn leaves from collecting on the bottom of the pool. As they decay, fallen leaves give off gases that dissolve in the water and can harm aquatic plants and fish.

To prevent leaves from getting into the water in the first place, you can cover the pool with a screen mounted on a wooden frame. Clean the screen at least once a week so that wet leaves do not become matted on the surface. For large ponds where such a frame may be impractical, use a heavy net suspended over the water surface and secured at the pool edges with rocks or boards. Dump the excess leaves before their weight pulls the net into the water.

A convenient way to remove leaves from the bottom of the pool is with a pool sweep powered by your garden hose. (These are available from mail-order suppliers.) Leaves sucked up by the sweep become trapped in a mesh bag, which you must empty periodically. Fish will not be sucked into the pool sweep since they will flee to the far side of the pool during sweeping; if snails get sucked up accidentally, you'll see or feel them in the bag and can remove them. Be sure to add dechlorinating compounds to the water before you use the pool sweep.

If a garden pool containing fish is completely covered by ice for more than a few days, the fish may suffocate because gases get trapped beneath the ice. This happens more quickly when decaying plant debris lies on the bottom of the pool. The fish need only a small air hole. There are several ways you can prevent a pool from icing over completely.

In mildly cold regions you may be able to keep the surface of the pond ice-free all winter by placing a circulating pump on the bottom, where the water is warmer, and discharging the water 2 or 3 inches below the surface. Where the cold is more severe, install a thermostatically controlled de-icer.

Another method of preventing ice formation in mildly cold climates is to build a protective frame of wood covered with clear PVC.

Mail-Order Sources

If possible, purchase plants and supplies from your local nursery, where you can inspect your purchases and don't have to pay shipping charges. But if you can't locate the plants or materials you want locally, these mail-order sources specialize in water gardening plants and equipment.

Lilypons Water Gardens
Box 10
Lilypons, MD 21717-0010
Plants, fish, books, and equipment

Paradise Water Gardens
62 May Street
Whitman, MA 02382
Plants, books, and equipment

Santa Barbara Water Gardens
Box 4353
Santa Barbara, CA 93140
Plants, books, and equipment

Slocum Water Gardens
1101 Cypress Gardens Boulevard
Winter Haven, FL 33880-6099
Plants, books, fish, and equipment

Tetra Pond
Box 4858
Toms River, NJ 08754-9946
PVC liners and equipment

Van Ness Water Gardens
2460 North Euclid
Upland, CA 91786-1199
Plants, fish, books, and equipment

Waterford Gardens
74 East Allendale Road
Saddle River, NJ 07458
Plants, fish, books, and equipment

Emergency Measures

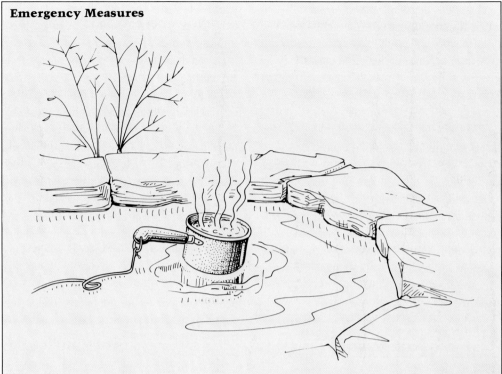

Where freezing is a rare occurrence, you can melt a breathing hole for the fish in an iced-over pool by setting a pot of boiling water on the ice. Tie a string to the pot handle so you can easily retrieve the pot if it falls through.

Place this plastic roof over one end of the pond as an insulator. The heat of the sun shining through the clear plastic will prevent ice from forming, except under the most extreme conditions. Be sure to allow some space under the plastic so that air can circulate.

Where freezing is rare, you can take emergency measures by using a pot of hot water. Bring a pot full of water to a boil on your stove. Carry the pot to the pool and rest it on the surface of the ice. It will melt through the ice and provide a breathing hole. Be sure to tie a string to the pot in case it falls in as the ice melts. Repeat as necessary. Whatever you do, don't bash a hole in the ice: The fish will be killed by the shock waves.

In most areas, hardy fish can be kept in an outdoor pond throughout the entire winter, if the pond is set in the ground and not raised above it. In parts of the country where the water might freeze clear through, fish must be removed from the pond and brought indoors. Keep the fish in cool, well-aerated water that is properly treated to remove chlorine compounds.

Tender aquatic plants that you bring indoors should be kept in a greenhouse pool all winter. Some, such as dwarf papyrus, may be kept as houseplants if their containers are submerged in water.

SEASONAL CARE IN WARM CLIMATES

In warm climates, the garden pool never goes completely dormant. Tropical water lilies may bloom until December and fish will only be inactive if the water temperature falls below 45° F. You will need to keep on feeding the fish as long as they appear active. Continue fertilizing the water lilies until December but stop feeding the other aquatics in October.

Siphon off leaves and other debris in late fall or early winter and, once a week, cut off plant parts in need of grooming. Clean pump screens and filters regularly and be sure that the water remains topped up.

CONTROLLING AQUATIC WEEDS AND PESTS

In garden pools, floating and submerged plants often grow so abundantly that they must be thinned out to keep some water surface open. You can pull excess plants out by hand or with a plastic garden rake. If you keep an eye on these plants and do not let them get out of control, your weeding task will require only a few minutes a week.

A number of insects (fewer than those found elsewhere in your garden) are fond of eating aquatic plants. With close observation you will be able to spot the pests. You can pick off caterpillars by hand; wade into the pool wearing wading boots to reach plants, if necessary. Other small pests can be washed away by pushing the leaves underwater or spraying with a stream from a hose.

Most insecticides shouldn't be used near the water, since they can harm fish. BT (*Bacillus thuringiensis*), a bacteria pathogenic to young larvae, is safe to use on all caterpillars and worms. This is available under many brand names; follow directions on the label. Some water gardeners use a vegetable oil on

aquatic plants to smother insects. The most common pests troubling aquatic plants are described below.

China Mark Moths

Large oval holes, cut marks, cutting or shredding in the foliage of aquatic plants, especially of water lilies, are signs of China mark moth caterpillars. There are two kinds, the beautiful China mark moth, and the brown China mark moth. The caterpillars feed on the under and upper sides of leaves and bind cut pieces of leaves around themselves with silk. They also bore into leaf stems, killing the leaves. Damage inflicted by these pests is unsightly, but not serious enough to kill the plants. Caterpillars can easily be picked off by hand, or controlled with BT if you catch them while they are still small.

Pump Maintenance

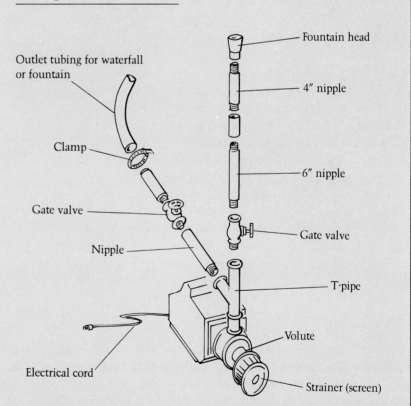

Because it is sealed and self-lubricating, a submersible pump generally needs no maintenance. If there is a manufacturing flaw, it is usually around the engine seal and the pump may leak oil. If oil does get into your pool, you can absorb it from the water surface with floating newspapers. Most pumps are covered by a one-year warranty, and may be returned for a replacement if leaks are caused by manufacturing defects. In alkaline water, corrosion may ruin the pump.

It is important at all times to make sure that the water passage is free. If the intake area or intake screen become clogged with sediment or debris, water flow is restricted and the motor may run dry, heat up, and burn out. You must clean the screen regularly.

At the outflow area, water passes through a volute, a long, cone-shaped nozzle that is inserted into the tubing. Occasionally, debris may become clogged in the volute, which houses the impeller. (The impeller is the whirring fan blade that actually pushes the water through the outflow.) If this should occur, unplug the pump and remove the screen covering the volute. Direct a strong stream of water through the volute to dislodge the object. Use a small brush or stream of water to remove any foreign matter clogging the volute. Algae that builds up in

this area should also be scrubbed away.

When the pump is running constantly, the intake screen or filter should be cleaned no less than once a month. Clean it more frequently if leaves or sediment tend to collect on the bottom of

the pond. Under no circumstances should the motor be run when the intake is above water or when the pond is dry, as this will cause it to burn out. It is also inadvisable to start and stop the motor frequently.

Labels in diagram: Outlet tubing for waterfall or fountain · Clamp · Gate valve · Nipple · Electrical cord · Fountain head · 4″ nipple · 6″ nipple · Gate valve · T-pipe · Volute · Strainer (screen)

False Leaf-mining Midge

A narrow tracery of lines appearing on the upper surface of water lily foliage is a sign of false leaf-mining midges. The midges lay eggs in the foliage and the larvae form mines or tunnels in the leaves. Pick off infested leaves and destroy them to prevent the pest from spreading.

Waterlily Aphid

The waterlily aphid is especially prevalent during warm, humid weather, when it attacks leaves and flowers. The small wingless insects reproduce prolifically, causing disfigured growth and spreading virus diseases. To control them, hose foliage with water. If any are left behind, submerge the infested flowers and pads and shake them underwater to remove the pests. An active fish population will take care of the ones that are dislodged.

In severe infestations, some gardeners spray with a mixture of corn oil and water. The oil should smother the pests without harming fish. Do not spray new leaves when the temperature is over 80° F.

FISH PREDATORS AND DISEASES

Two types of beetles occasionally attack and kill fish in garden ponds. The great diving beetle measures about 1½ inches long and ¾ inch wide. Its body is dark brown and tinged brownish gold. The beetle attaches itself to the body of a fish and feeds off its juices. Since they must surface periodically to breathe, you can net the pests with a hand net and destroy them.

Water boatmen beetles swim on their backs on the surface, using their legs like oars to speed themselves across the water. They can inflict wounds on large fish and kill the fry. Frequent netting is the only way to dispose of these pests.

Fish diseases may be caused by bacteria, fungi, or parasites and can kill fish if they are not treated. Often, overstocking or dirty water causes the fish to weaken, which leads to disease. Fish under stress are particularly susceptible to disease. Stress may be caused by transportation, low oxygen supply, high ammonia content in the water, improper water pH, sudden temperature or pH change, and improper diet.

Disease symptoms are not difficult for a beginner to observe. If you see a fish that is blotched or discolored, remove it immediately. A number of general fish medicines are available for parasite, fungus, and bacterial control. You may want to keep these at hand. Consult a book or local fish dealer for help in choosing the correct treatment.

If there are too many fish in the pond, waste builds up in the form of ammonia, which leads to gradual poisoning. Gases given off by excessive leaf decay can also cause fish to weaken and die. The best remedy in either case is to remove the fish, change the water, and reduce the population before returning the healthy fish to the fresh pond water.

Most of the routine care needed by your water garden won't take much of your time. As you're enjoying the pool, you'll clip a dead blossom here, a pad there, add a bit of water from the garden hose, and wash off a few pests at the same time. Part of the enjoyment of your pool comes from the involvement you feel in tending it. And that comes naturally.

It takes only a few minutes a week to snip off faded flowers or yellowed leaves; regular grooming keeps your garden pool looking its best.

Climate Zone Map

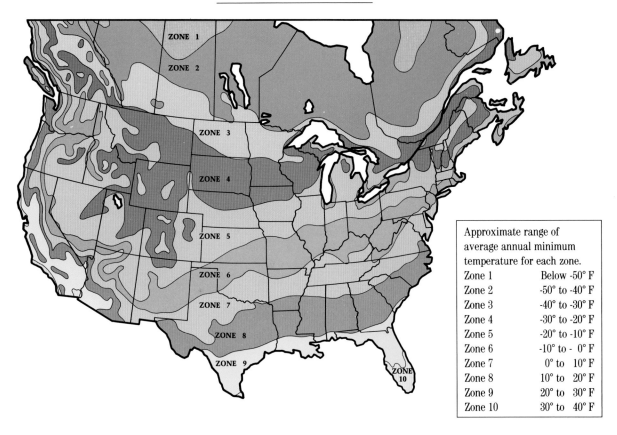

Approximate range of
average annual minimum
temperature for each zone.

Zone 1	Below -50° F
Zone 2	-50° to -40° F
Zone 3	-40° to -30° F
Zone 4	-30° to -20° F
Zone 5	-20° to -10° F
Zone 6	-10° to - 0° F
Zone 7	0° to 10° F
Zone 8	10° to 20° F
Zone 9	20° to 30° F
Zone 10	30° to 40° F

U.S. Measure and Metric Measure Conversion Chart

		Formulas for Exact Measures			Rounded Measures for Quick Reference		
	Symbol	When you know:	Multiply by:	To find:			
Mass	oz	ounces	28.35	grams	1 oz		= 30 g
(Weight)	lb	pounds	0.45	kilograms	4 oz		= 115 g
	g	grams	0.035	ounces	8 oz		= 225 g
	kg	kilograms	2.2	pounds	16 oz	= 1 lb	= 450 g
					32 oz	= 2 lb	= 900 g
					36 oz	= 2¼ lb	= 1000g (1 kg)
Volume	pt	pints	0.47	liters	1 c	= 8 oz	= 250 ml
	qt	quarts	0.95	liters	2 c (1 pt)	= 16 oz	= 500 ml
	gal	gallons	3.785	liters	4 c (1 qt)	= 32 oz	= 1 liter
	ml	milliliters	0.034	fluid ounces	4 qt (1 gal)	= 128 oz	= 3¾ liter
Length	in.	inches	2.54	centimeters	⅜ in.		= 1 cm
	ft	feet	30.48	centimeters	1 in.		= 2.5 cm
	yd	yards	0.9144	meters	2 in.		= 5 cm
	mi	miles	1.609	kilometers	2½ in.		= 6.5 cm
	km	kilometers	0.621	miles	12 in. (1 ft)		= 30 cm
	m	meters	1.094	yards	1 yd		= 90 cm
	cm	centimeters	0.39	inches	100 ft		= 30 m
					1 mi		= 1.6 km
Temperature	°F	Fahrenheit	⅝ (after subtracting 32)	Celsius	32°F		= 0°C
	°C	Celsius	⅝ (then add 32)	Fahrenheit	212°F		= 100°C
Area	in.²	square inches	6.452	square centimeters	1 in.²		= 6.5 cm²
	ft²	square feet	929.0	square centimeters	1 ft²		= 930 cm²
	yd²	square yards	8361.0	square centimeters	1 yd²		= 8360 cm²
	a.	acres	0.4047	hectares	1 a.		= 4050 m²